Secrets of
GOOD LIVING

Secrets of
GOOD LIVING

Dr. Brij Bhushan Goel
D.Ph., NDDY, PGDHHC, Ph.D.

STERLING

STERLING PAPERBACKS
An imprint of
Sterling Publishers (P) Ltd.
Regd. Office: A-59, Okhla Industrial Area, Phase-II,
New Delhi-110020. CIN: U22110PB1964PTC002569
Tel: 26387070, 26386209; Fax: 91-11-26383788
E-mail: mail@sterlingpublishers.com
www.sterlingpublishers.com

Secrets of Good Living

ISBN 978 81 207 7993 8
Reprint 2014

Printed in India

Printed and Published by Sterling Publishers Pvt. Ltd.,
New Delhi-110 020.

Alertness in observing opportunity, courage, and the ability to grab opportunity; firm determination to achieve success through opportunity; and the patience to do the work unless complete, are strong qualities through which success is definitely achieved.

Contents

Preface	xi
Secrets of Healthy Living	1
The Art of Laughing and Smiling	13
Human Nature	15
Human Powers	16
Positive Thinking	18
Creative Thinking	23
Group Discussions	26
The Power of Praise	27
Personality Development	28
First Impression	29
The Ability To Adjust	31
The Power of Love	33
Friendship	35
Mental Block	38
Superstition (Blind Faith)	39
Depression	43
Work and Destiny	47
The Art of Learning	52
Importance of Books	54
Anger Management	55
Rectification of Mistakes	64
Failure To Succeed	65
Problems and Their Solutions	66
Intoxication Is A Curse	69

Jealousy	78
Criticism	80
Effect of Society (Company)	82
Falsehood and Truth	83
Enmity	85
Loneliness	87
Boredom	89
Fear	91
Hesitation	94
Hurry and Rashness	95
Unnecessary Interference	97
Mobile	99
Television	101
Languor of Spirit	102
Uncontrolled Ambitions	104
Dissatisfaction	106
Character Formation	107
Patience	108
Forgiveness	109
Morality	110
The Art of Donation	111
Correct Decisions	117
Habits	120
Resolution	122
Social Service	123
Social Relations	126
Self-Motivation	127
Self-Control	129
Self-Confidence	131
Self-Analysis	135

Enhance Soft Skills 137
Professional/Professionalism 138
Workaholic 140
Rest 141
Pleasure 142
Entertainment 144
Responsibility 146
Effective Leadership 148
Time Management 149
Art of Communication 154
Science of Giving 158
As You Give So You Receive 159
Ego (Pride) 160
Advice 162
Learn To Say No 163
Public Speaking 165
Art of Listening 167
Body Language 169
A Successful Manager 174
Job Interview 176
Make Your Employees The Best 178
Importance of Remembering Names 179
Accept The Changes 180
Turn Your Arranged Marriage Into A Love Marriage 182
Family Planning 186
Development of Children 188
Girl Child — Curse or Blessing 191
The Importance of Parents 194
Relationships 197
Generation Gap 206

Old Age – Curse or Boon 209
Stress Management 219
The Power of Thought 226
Mind Power 228
A Positive Attitude 236
Set Your Goal 239
Priority 242
Success 243
Life Means Moving On... 247
Passion 248
Having The Safety Shield of Insurance 249
The Necessity of Nomination 256
Good Salesman 258
What People Want 260
Win The Customer 261
Financial Planning 263
Make Your Will 270
Green Living 277
Love For The Nation 282
Human Religion 292
Self-Realisation 294
Prayer 295
Liberation 296

Preface

Are we actually living a life or are we just alive? We enter this world crying, keep complaining throughout our lives, and ultimately die in despair.

Learn to live life in such a way that your whole life becomes fragrant.

Good living means following a lifestyle that is full of fresh beliefs and ideas, and one that includes the enthusiasm and the thrill to better what is already available to you. After all, it is we who are responsible for creating the kind of life we wish to lead. So let's try and put in the effort of making it beautiful and precious.

It is rightly said that we get just one life to live and so we should live it fully. But this is easier said than done. Most of us are stuck between our high aspirations and the burden of reality. Life becomes a strain and we are overwhelmed by the feelings of failure, depression, and loneliness. To prevent such a state, we need to learn to live our lives by striking a proper balance between our family, friends, professional life, and personal needs. This can be achieved by adopting a proper co-ordination between our physical, mental, economical, and spiritual condition.

We all possess two types of life – one which we live on the outside and the other that is inside us but can't be lived. It is obvious that the latter is the one that is needed to be known and understood. Along with this it is also necessary to know what exactly is a successful life. Different people can have differing opinions about it. For some a successful life may mean to live in a secure and enjoyable place, and enjoy the company and respect of near and dear ones. For some a successful life could consist of actions and tasks undertaken that contribute to immense personal satisfaction, while for some a prosperous life could be one that is filled with money and goods to satisfy one's personal needs. Then there are some who may think that a successful life means living in such a society that protects every individual's freedom.

To better understand this, observe the lives of the CEOs of multinational companies or the way prominent industrialists live their lives. They remain tense under the pressure of setting and achieving new goals. By looking at their status, fame, and wealth we assume that they are happy, but this is far from the real picture. Generally such people are victims of disorders, such as depression, high blood pressure (hypertension), migraine, heart disease, or indigestion. They cannot be called happy because one who is unhealthy cannot be happy. These people are only concerned about themselves and their targets. Failure makes them sad and depressed whereas success gives them happiness and confidence. The thing is that they do not have just one aim but a wheel of aims and when this wheel rotates their excitement, tension, greed, and wants increase, thus making them prone to frustration.

Generally when a businessman goes for enjoyment to a tourist place then even there he cannot get rid of his mobile through which he keeps himself updated about his business developments and also uses it to give instructions. He does not have time to feel the cool breeze, to hear the sweet sound of waterfall, or to listen to the sound of flowing water.

We all live desiring big success and happiness. We all want that whatever we get should be big. But actually in order to achieve big happiness we often overlook countless chances full of small happiness. If we learn to adopt and share those small moments of happiness then our life will be full of joy.

One who does not make proper use of happiness and sorrow deteriorates his condition.

It's a natural phenomenon that happiness if not used properly decreases and sorrow if not used properly increases.

A wise person does not repent on the past, is ready to face tomorrow without fear and confidently makes proper use of today. Those who walk by themselves reach their destination but those who walk with their brain reach their destiny.

The nutritional value of food remains the same irrespective of the type of utensil used for eating it. Similarly if we have internal happiness then the amount of materialistic resource does not matter.

Happy people do not necessarily possess everything, they obtain happiness from whatever they have.

This book explains us how to remain healthy, be positive, improve our personality, remove our weakness, adopt goodness, convert other's negativity into positivity, obtain success, utilise mental strength, stay happily in a family, secure oneself financially, and also make old age a bliss so that we can enjoy life fully.

The main objective of writing this book is to make every person achieve success and happiness.

– Brij Bhushan Goel

Why is water not dirty –
because it keeps flowing.

Why doesn't any obstacle
come in the way of water –
because it keeps flowing.

Why does one drop of
water become a river
from a fountain, a big river
from a medium river,
and a sea from a big river –
because it keeps flowing.

So my life, do not stop;
keep moving.

Secrets of Healthy Living

To have a good standard of living, one should always try and stay healthy.

To be completely healthy one has to be physically, mentally, socially, emotionally, and spiritually fit.

If a person is suffering from various physical ailments, then he is considered to be physically unhealthy.

When a person has worries, tensions, and a negative approach towards life, then he is considered to be mentally unhealthy.

When a person quarrels with his near ones, relatives, and friends, then he is considered to be socially unhealthy.

When a person is full of anger, greed, empty pride, hatred, jealousy, etc., then he is considered to be emotionally unhealthy.

When a person is disturbed due to intimacy of love and affection, then he is considered to be spiritually unhealthy.

By adopting naturopathy and yoga one can get rid of all these ailments.

Naturopathy and yoga work like two wheels of a bicycle. There is no medical system that can even attempt to provide complete health.

Naturopathy

Naturopathy is not just a treatment; it is also a secret of healthy living.

With the practice of naturopathy, ailments are eradicated from their root. Other hidden problems are get cured. There are no side effects because no medicines are used.

Naturopathy works in two ways. First, it makes the patient get rid of his ailment speedily, and second it educates them on how to remain healthy in future.

When all treatments fail, naturopathy can still attempt a cure.

Cause of diseases

All the ailments of the human body have only one reason to occur – the accumulation of toxins (waste products) in the body.

Forms of waste products

1. The nutrients in the food get destroyed when it is cooked, fried, or roasted and waste products continue to increase in the food.
2. Air pollution is also a major reason for the waste products to enter the body through breathing.
3. Various physical and chemical reactions occur in the human body, and the by-products of these reactions are also called waste products.
4. In the body, continuous replacement of cells takes place; old cells die and new ones take their place. The destroyed cells contribute to the waste products present in the body.
5. Some waste products are produced in the body because of the occurrence of chemical changes that the body undergoes during episodes of fear, tension, anger, jealousy, stress, negativity, etc.

Reasons for accumulation of waste products

Nature excretes waste products from the body, but at times they get accumulated. This may happen:

1. when the input of waste products through food is more than the output of waste products by the body.
2. there is some obstruction or blockage in any of the processes of waste excretion, namely, through the, stool, urine, sweat, and breath.

3. some acute diseases, such as fever, diarrhoea, vomiting, influenza, cough, etc., are interrupted and suppressed by medicines. These diseases happen when toxins in the body increase; various parts of the body become non-functional, and the immune system weakens. Nature discards these toxins from the body in the form of these disease processes.

Some of the waste products in the body are generated at the following sites:

(i) **Stool:** When stool gets stuck in the intestine and ferments, it produces toxins and gases. The intestine secretes enzymes for the digestion of the food. Because the intestine is obstructed by the stool, there is not enough secretion of the enzymes and hence digestion gets hampered. This results in less absorption of nutrients, such as minerals, vitamins, etc., in the body which then becomes nutrient deficient.

(ii) **Urine:** The kidneys filter blood and produce urine using the resultant waste products in the body and the water present. Deficiency of water or intake of excess salt blocks the filtration process of the kidneys, and as a result the waste products get retained in the blood.

(iii) **Sweat:** The skin too excretes waste products which is in the form of sweat. If the pores of the skin are blocked, the waste products remain in the body.

(iv) **Breath:** The respiratory system excretes volatile waste products (carbon dioxide, etc.) from the body. If deep breaths are not taken during the process of respiration, there is less expansion of the lungs; hence, the intake of oxygen is reduced which leads to the less excretion of carbon dioxide as well.

A common cure for all diseases

For all diseases there is one cure, and that is the detoxification of the body by natural means.

By following this system of treatment, not only is one disease cured but the whole body is treated, holistically.

Natural means of detoxifying the body:

i **Fasting**: This is the best way of maintaining good health or rejuvenating one's body and essential for treating both patients as well as healthy individuals.

The main function of fasting is the process of detoxification of the body. During fasting our energy that is relieved from the task of digesting food, is utilised in extracting those elements that cause ailments in the body.

Fasting can be done for a day or for many days. It is a useful practice to fast once a week, if possible.

Ways of fasting: Do not take any kind of food throughout the day. Drink 2–2½ litres of water with the juice of 2–3 lemons in a day at short intervals. If this is not possible, fruit or vegetable juice can be consumed. Those who cannot fast completely may eat fruits once during each day of fasting.

Never break a fast by eating solid (heavy) food. When breaking a fast first take either orange juice, sweet lemon juice, grape juice, or whichever fruit or vegetable juice you prefer. A short-duration fast can be broken by eating fruits.

These days people break fasts by eating heavy (fried and oily) food that proves harmful rather than being nutritious and beneficial.

ii **Uncooked food**: Uncooked food simply means eating food in an uncooked form, as per our capacity, that we otherwise consume after cooking. Foods such as fresh fruits, green leafy vegetables, salad, sprouts, dry fruits, etc., are some items that may be consumed in a raw and uncooked form.

To fight against any disease, and to live a healthy and happy life, uncooked food is one of the most powerful weapons that one can use (Brahma's *Astra*). Uncooked food is equivalent to nectar. By merely improving one's food intake and eating habits, many ailments can be easily cured.

Note: Dry fruits such as almonds, cashew nuts, groundnuts, raisins, figs, black raisins, dry dates should always be soaked in water before consumption.

Avoid using salt in eatables, such as fruits, salads, sprouts, and juices.

iii **Morning water drink**: Drink up to four glasses of water kept overnight in a silver or copper vessel before using the washroom in the morning. When practiced daily it prevents various diseases from attacking the body.

iv **Mud pack**: It is very useful in all ailments of the abdomen. The pack can be applied on the lower abdomen, chest, forehead, eyes, head, spine, throat, feet, anus, and wherever else needed.

v **Enema**: In the world of healing, this is considered the safest way of cleansing the intestines, and it gives relief from constipation.

vi **Hip bath**: It gives permanent relief from all ailments of the abdomen and is beneficial in almost all other forms of illnesses.

vii **Steam bath**: It unclogs the pores of the skin, which then excretes toxins from the body. This method too is useful in almost all ailments of the body.

viii **Hot foot bath**: Helps in fighting cold, cough, blood pressure, unconsciousness, and attacks of asthma. Women going through menopause benefit immensely from this bath if taken regularly for long periods.

ix **Spinal bath**: This helps when suffering from complaints such as high and low blood pressure (hypertension and hypotension), sleeplessness and insomnia, unconsciousness, fatigue, general weakness, and nervous tension. It also promotes and regulates blood circulation in the body.

x **Sitz bath**: Disorders such as premature ejaculation of semen, leucorrhoea, and nervous weakness all benefit from a sitz bath. Anger too is gradually cured by using this form of bathing. It is especially good for relieving pain from conditions such as neuralgia and sciatica. Most kinds of female ailments too are benefitted from its use.

xi **Hot and cold fomentation**: Alternate hot and cold fomentation is very useful to repair a part of the body or to bring relief in pain and no other treatment is as effective as this one. On the abdomen, hot and cold fomentation provides relief from chronic constipation, gastric trouble, and also removes weakness.

xii **Compress**: This is especially useful in thyroid and parathyroid problems, tonsillitis, asthma, liver problems, diabetes, kidney ailments, arthritis, varicose veins etc.

xiii *Kunjal*: This helps in disorders of the cheek, face (pimples), teeth, tongue, blood, chest, constipation, acidity, gastric, cough, night blindness, asthma, drying of the mouth, and throat, etc.

xiv **Wet sheet pack**: This is used to get relief in fever, to strengthen nerve tissues, and extract waste products from the body. After use, the sheet produces an offensive smell because of all the waste that it extracts from the body. The more the toxic wastes come out of the body, the more pale yellowish colour the sheet obtains.

xv *Jalneti*: All ailments related to the organs above the neck (headache, sleeplessness, excessive sleep, falling of hair, boils or protruded flesh growth within the nose (polyps), cold, runny nose, eye complications, hearing problems, epilepsy, etc.) are cured.

xvi **Chromotherapy**: The rays of the sun are a combination of seven colours, and each colour has separate medicinal properties that can be absorbed in the water, honey, ghee, oil, etc., for desired benefits (water for drinking, honey, ghee for massage of spinal cord, oil for other external use).

xvii **Looking at the rising sun**: By fixing the eyes towards the ruddy glow of the rising sun, eye diseases are cured.

xviii **Sun bath**: Sunbathing strengthens weak bones, eases dental problems, aids with weak digestion, and provides relief to the diseases of the nerves and muscles.

Yoga

The following are the eight parts of Yoga:
1)Yama 2)Niyama 3)Asana 4)Pranayama 5)Pratyahara 6) Dharana 7)Dhyan 8)Samadhi.

(1) **Yama** (behaviour): Yama leads to a true and good behaviour towards others. It has five parts:

(i) *Ahimsa* (non-violence): To avoid afflicting pain on anyone in thought, speech, or action.

(ii) *Satya* (truthfulness): One should be simple and clear and not treacherous in one's behaviour.

(iii) *Asteya* (non-stealing): Not stealing anything from anyone is asteya. Not paying appropriate wages for a task done is also considered stealing.

(iv) *Brahmacharya* (celibacy): All sensual pleasures be given up mentally, in speech, and physically under all circumstances is brahmacharya.

(v) *Aparigraha* (non-hoarding): To restrain one's self from the collection of materialistic things.

(2) **Niyama** (regulations): Niyamas are connected with the individual's body, senses, and conscience. By adhering to them regularly the mind becomes truthful, pure, and grand. Niyama also has five parts:

(i) *Shauch* (cleanliness): Internal and external cleanliness of the body.

(ii) *Santosh* (contentment): Contentment in the fruit you reap.

(iii) *Tapa* (dutifulness): Perform your duty with diligence.

(iv) *Svadhyaya* (regular practice): Regular study of one's own life; this enables an individual to understand his own duties and responsibilities.

(v) *Ishwar pranidhan* (surrenders to God): Seek refuge in the Lord.

(3). **Asana** (Yogasana): Asana (postures) is connected with physical activity. This gets rid of restlessness, instability, laziness, and obesity and provides *satvik* glow and grandeur. Nowhere in the world has any other activity been found to be as effective as the Asanas for ailments of the endocrine glands

(4) **Pranayama**: It increases resistance power and creates a sense of peace, pleasure, and longevity.

(5) **Pratyahara**: When anything is perceived by the senses, then to control the various sense organs is called pratyahara. It gives the power of controlling.

(6) **Dharana**: Helps in achieving one's goal in life.

(7) **Dhyan**: Regular practice of this removes nervous weakness and increases memory, foresightedness, creative thinking, and problem solving skills.

(8) **Samadhi**: This leads to a state where the mortal soul is said to have merged with the universal soul; it is also known as achieving *moksha*.

Healthy Thoughts – A disease incurable by all medical systems can be cured merely by the feeling of being healthy.

Adopt the following habits for a healthy living

1. Immediately after waking up fill the mouth with clean water and sprinkle water on both eyes, if possible, forty times. This prevents weakening of the eyesight and gets rid of spectacles.
2. To prevent diseases of the throat, do saline gargles daily
3. While brushing teeth or taking a bath, clean the palate (upper part inside mouth) with the thumb. This prevents ailments of eye, nose, and throat.
4. While urinating or evacuating the bowels, press the jaws tight; this strengthens the teeth and tooth ailments do not occur.
5. Avoid eating or drinking anything that is too hot or too cold, because this is extremely harmful for digestion.
6. Do not eat when stricken with worries and grief, or when tired or angry.
7. Maintain a gap of 5–6 hours between meals, and eat dinner three hours before sleeping.
8. Do not drink water while eating. Water should be consumed either 30 minutes before or 40–60 minutes after a meal.
9. Avoid watching television during meals; try and concentrate on the food being eaten and enjoy the meal.
10. Wash and rinse the mouth after eating or drinking any food stuff at any time.

Difference between yogasana and exercise

In the posture of yogasana, staying in a posture is a must by gradually increasing the time of hold. The more time one will stay in a posture the more will be the benefit. If one does not stay in a specific posture then it is called an exercise.

Yogasana	Exercise
1. Yogasana when done regularly affects even the smallest part of the body.	1. The process of doing exercises generally affects only a particular part of the body.
2. Yogasana provides flexibility to the body.	2. Exercises provide stiffness to the body.
3. The internal energy of the body is used less while doing yogasana.	3. There is more use of the internal energy while exercising.
4. Yogasana helps cure ailments.	4. Exercises alone cannot cure ailments of the body.
5. Mental and physical fatigue is eliminated in yogasana.	5. Exercises cause physical fatigue.
6. Yogasana does not cause any harm to any part of the body.	6. At times exercising may cause more harm than good.
7. Yogasana aids in the proper development of the internal organs of the body and improves the functioning of the endocrine glands.	7. Exercise affects only the functional system of the muscles and bones.
8. Yogasana restores the lost energy of the body.	8. Exercise does not lead to the restoration of lost energy of the body while exercising.
9. Yogasana helps in physical as well as mental and emotional development.	9. Exercise helps only in the physical development of the body.
10. Yogasana can be done by any person of any age.	10. Rigorous exercise can only be done by young individuals. Harsh and strenuous exercises should not be attempted by aged people.

Morning Walk

Morning walk is a natural exercise and proves extremely beneficial to the body. There is no age limit for a person to go for a morning walk. Any person between the age of 4 and 100 years can go for a morning walk. An evening walk can also be advantageous.

Benefits of morning walk

- It helps in exercising the entire body
- It aids in digestion
- It reduces depression and peevishness
- It makes the brain active and vibrant
- It relaxes the body and gives a fresh and energetic feeling
- It helps in reducing or maintaining weight
- It reduces the risk of heart-related ailments and paralysis
- It reduces high blood pressure and high blood cholesterol
- It makes the bones stronger and reduces the risk of osteoporosis
- It reduces the chance of arthritis
- It makes the body flexible, which in turn reduces the chances of receiving injuries

It is advisable not to start jogging at once. First start walking slowly, gradually increase the speed and then reach up to jogging.

Hence, regular morning walks for at least half an hour (2–3 km) daily are a must.

Identification of a diseased body

The following indications are found in a body that is ailing:

- Any abnormality in physical activity.

- Lack of sound sleep.
- Stool is either loose or in lumps.
- Loss of appetite.
- Belly protrudes out as compared to the chest.
- Body tires easily. Continuous creation of negative thoughts.
- Short-tempered.
- Lethargic body.
- Addiction to intoxicating products.
- Weight issues: obese, overweight, underweight, etc.

If any of these indications are ignored or suitable treatment is avoided, these ailments have a tendency to become chronic and deep-seated.

Detoxification of the body results in rejuvenation and the body is full of new life again. The individual feels confident and ready to undertake new endeavours.

Suggestion

Contact Nature Cure & Yoga Centre and adopt detoxification of body and natural diet.

The causes of diseases are not in our body, only the results are found there. The causes are actually in our incorrect way of living — lifestyle.

The Art of Laughing and Smiling

Nature has given the best gift to mankind – that to laugh and smile. This precious boon to the humans brings with it happiness and peace.

Laughter is the best tonic for the body and smile is the best cosmetic.

No person is so broke that they cannot gift a smile to others. A smile brings with it radiance and beauty. Share the gift of a smile and make the world a better place.

We should not only make others laugh but should also learn to laugh at ourselves. Sharing a laugh helps cheer up our surroundings and creates a stress-free setting. To laugh and make other people laugh is a good thing, but to laugh at other people and make a mockery of them is rude and ungraceful.

The basic ingredient of success is happiness; try to remain happy in all phases of life no matter what. Difficulties do come from time to time, but success comes early only to that person who meets challenges head on with optimism and good humour. A cheerful person reaches his goal easily because of the positive attitude that he adopts to reach there. Jolly people are always successful in every step of their life; they have lots of friends and are very popular in their circle.

While laughing people forget all their differences and tend to come closer. In a relationship such as of husband and wife, if there are moments of laughter and happiness then the home becomes heaven.

Laughter can also be called the medicine for many diseases. There are so many ailments that can get cured by laughing loudly. When a person laughs, the body releases pain-relieving hormones that decrease the joint pains and muscular spasms. Laughter is also believed to be a treatment for memory loss.

When we laugh, the brain releases a chemical called endorphin; this chemical is considered good for health and helps control blood pressure, diabetes, obesity, etc. Laughter is also beneficial for the treatment for certain lung conditions, respiratory problems, and asthma.

Laughter is excellent for digestion. It reduces the levels of stress-related hormones, increases overall energy, and stimulates the balanced functioning of internal organs.

While laughing, the tear glands in the eyes contract and the eyes get watery, which brings a shine to the eyes.

A smile has the power to get rid of anxiety, anger, and negative thoughts.

Include laughter and pleasure into your lifestyle. Some people are not able to laugh loudly, but internal laughter too is effective. So, never give up the opportunity to laugh and to spread laughter and happiness. If you do not feel comfortable laughing in front of others, do it when you are alone or in front of a mirror in the privacy of your bathroom. Nowadays, many "Laughter Clubs" have opened in various cities and towns that help people in forgetting their day-to-day problems and encourage them to laugh with full enthusiasm. Include smiling and laughing in your daily routine and see your troubles and stress vanish.

Happiness and success cannot be got by materialistic possessions. They always come from within a person. Always try to be happy even in sorrowful moments. By doing this the mind is filled with splendour and abundance. The immune system of the body gets stronger and the process of ageing becomes slow.

A person who laughs and spreads happiness around him can never commit a crime. Laughter can surely be used to control criminal activity in the society and reduce the ever-increasing numbers of offences.

Human Nature

When dealing with individuals, keep in mind the following points:

1. All human beings are alike.
2. All humans are different.
3. People pay incomplete attention.
4. People respond to good sentiments.
5. People react best under pressure (deadlines).
6. People like formulas.
7. People resist change.
8. People like personal identification; their name printed, spelled, and pronounced correctly.
9. People like to have their opinions heard.
10. People want to be comfortable.
11. People like to avoid effort.
12. People like to be appreciated.
13. People are suspicious of perfection.
14. Everybody has ego and self-respect.
15. Everybody has wants.
16. Everybody has habits.
17. Everybody respects leadership.
18. Everybody is sexed.
19. Everybody has fears.
20. Everybody wants security.

Human Powers

Every living creature, human or beast, that exists on the Earth has powers. There is no living creature in this world that does not possess any power. Living or non-living, everyone and everything has its own power. Most people are not aware of their powers and many others do not know how to effectively utilise their powers. Instead of realising the strength of the power they possess, they find themselves feeling weak and powerless.

Human beings have immense power within themselves, but it is tragic and unfortunate that most of their powers lie dormant. Entire lives are spent without recognising the infinite powers and the unlimited possibilities that one possesses. Because of this many of our physical and mental powers are not used adequately, and our valuable spiritual powers lie mostly unspent.

There are two aspects to human powers — destructive and constructive. Every person has two different kinds of energy: positive energy and negative energy. Some use their powers constructively and some use their powers destructively.

Individuals who use their powers productively enjoy success and satisfaction in their lives, while individuals who make destructive use of their powers lead a life of suffering and distress.

The following are some of the Invaluable Powers that individuals possess:

Thought Power	Emotional Power
Tolerance Power	Decision Power
Will Power	Pardoning Power

Imagination Power
Spiritual Power
Word Power
Attraction Power
Selection Power
Positive Power
Hard working Power
Organisational Power
Vital (*Kundalini*) Power

Positive Thinking

In this world nothing is good or bad. It is our thinking that makes things good or bad. Our perception leads us to attach good or evil, positive or negative properties to everything in the world. To be able to notice good qualities and righteousness in situations or individuals is considered positive thinking and to merely notice flaws and worthlessness in everything is surely negative thinking.

Positive thinking makes us stress free and gives us a fresher outlook of life. Negative thinking makes us feel stressed out, frustrated, and disappointed with life in general.

Positive thoughts lead us to the mountain of excellence and negative thoughts drown us in the drain of evil.

Positive thoughts give rise to positive emotions such as mercy, love, compassion, forgiveness, gratitude, blissfulness, tolerance, faith, generosity, and hope.

Negative thoughts increase our fears and magnify bad qualities such as anger, hatred, jealousy, sadism, worry, intolerance, doubt, selfishness, and hopelessness.

A person with a healthy mind sees the good qualities in the other person, while a person with a contaminated mind sees only flaws in the other person.

As described in the epic Mahabharata, Yudhishthir never saw any ill in any person because his thoughts were pure and positive, whereas his cousin Duryodhana was never able to find or notice any good in any person because he was a slave to his negative thoughts.

A successful person always tries to see the positive side of things no matter how worse the situation or person. If we do not keep a positive attitude towards our life and activities, we will fail to get results in our favour.

Take for instance a door-to-door salesman; if he retreats from the door of a possible buyer without trying to persuade him to buy his product, thinking that the buyer may not purchase then he will never be able to sell and will obviously be a failure. Here it is his negative thinking that is responsible for his downfall.

Similarly, a person who thinks that he is ill will surely fall sick even if there are no symptoms of any particular ailment.

Through negative thinking we lose 95% of our energy; hence our biggest enemy is the cluster of negative thoughts in our head. The road to success becomes easier if we carry out our activities happily accompanied by a positive attitude.

Advantages of Positive Thinking

1. Stress levels become less.
2. There is a feeling of happiness and contentment in every situation.
3. Good relationships in the family and society are maintained.
4. There is a healthy development in one's personality and character.
5. One reaches the heights of success.
6. One is able to tackle problems without causing undue tension, because positive thinking teaches the art of finding solutions to problems in a reasonable and practical manner.
7. Positive encouragement makes an evil person a better person.
8. Each one of us possesses some unique qualities that others may not have, and having a positive attitude gives us the power to recognise those qualities.
9. A person with a positive attitude is never sad or disappointed.

10. The capacity to work increases.
11. Patience and self-confidence increase.
12. The decision-making capability also increases.
13. A creative way of thinking develops.
14. A positive attitude increases the health-protecting hormones in the body that in turn strengthen the immune system and make us healthy.
15. People with a positive attitude do not depend on others for their happiness; they create an atmosphere of joy and happiness around themselves.

How To Increase Positive Attitude

1. The true ability of a person is put to test in adverse situations. Treat such situations practically and do not allow them to control your life. Such situations do not last for long.
2. Make your critic your friend – they actually do good for us in our life, because it is their criticism that makes us recognise our shortcomings and forces us to work properly.
3. View every circumstance as an opportunity to learn something new, instead of criticising and feeling frustrated.
4. Try and believe this ideology – Adopt that which is suitable and leave that which is unsuitable.
5. Obstacles in life teach a person how to live life bravely.
6. Accept changes because change is the rule of nature.
7. Try and focus on the positive aspects and good qualities in an individual or a situation, instead of finding fault and noticing drawbacks.
8. Love whatever work you do and make continuous efforts to do it better.

9. Greet a guest with happiness and good humour; avoid discussing depressing issues at work or in family.
10. Take interest in other people's ideas and lives, and welcome their point of view and opinion.
11. Place yourself in the other person's circumstances and then try to take a decision.
12. Be optimistic.
13. Stop blaming others.
14. Ignore small and trivial things.
15. When faced with a hurdle, either find out a solution or else create one.
16. Failure is the ladder to success. A child learns to walk only after falling down a number of times.
17. Stay away from negative and sadist people.
18. Believe that whatever God does is always good. By adopting this mental attitude, you will be forced to find some goodness in all circumstances.
19. Develop the habit of encouraging others, no matter what the circumstance.
20. Try to always use kind and positive language while talking or writing.
21. Read good books and make an attempt to meet people from all walks of life so that you may get to learn something from them.
22. Avoid walking with your head hanging down; such a posture is a sign of negativity.
23. Whenever a negative thought enters your mind, say "No" to it or convert it into a positive one.
24. Always recognise the following:
    - I am satisfied with my life.
    - I am happy with myself.

- I will try and try again until I succeed.
- I am my own best friend.
- I am a cooperative person, and if I cooperate with others I too will get cooperation.
- I am focussed on my goal.
- I am a unique person and lead a typical life.
- To achieve success in life is solely in my hands.
- I will definitely be successful.

When a person finds faults or drawbacks in you for no reason, use your good behaviour and prove him wrong.

Creative Thinking

To be able to produce fresh thoughts, consider new concepts, and search for new solutions to obstacles, is the process of thinking creatively. Creative thinking sharpens the intellect and reduces mental stress.

It is the power of intellect that differentiates human beings from animals. The test of man's intellect is his ability to overcome difficult situations easily.

A person without any decision-making ability is one who has not practiced creative thinking, because it is thought that a person with intellect must necessarily think.

Develop your potential to ideate and solve complications yourself; the solution is within you.

It is your thinking alone that decides your attitude and response. For instance if you spend an hour trying to understand a situation logically and practically, it may save you valuable hours later when you attempt doing that particular work.

In an attempt to not be seen differently, we make futile efforts to emulate or copy others. Everyone in this world has something unique to offer about themselves. If you do a self-analysis and concentrate on your tasks without paying attention to what others are doing or thinking about you, it is guaranteed that you will be able to excel at your work. Try and draw attention to your own special qualities for which the world is waiting. Your unique quality could be your recognition – because you are you. No one can be completely identical to you in this world. You may even be rewarded by the world for possessing that unique quality. Be a risk taker and explore. Opportunities are waiting to be grabbed.

When we succeed in a particular task, it means it is time to move on and shift focus in another direction. Change is fun and full of learning. If our struggle is not continued, it leads to stagnation and decline.

Ways of Creative Thinking

1. Take an object of daily use and start thinking what could be its other uses. This can be turned into a group game too.
2. Take up a problem and try and find various solutions to it.
3. Find a way to reach a particular destination or make a new way for it.
4. Analyse your failures and think of some other better ways that might have been put to use to overcome the obstacles.
5. First decide and fix your goal; this is very important in life. Then with full commitment and determination pursue it. This process will force you to think creatively.
6. Organise a study circle along with some individuals and together exchange ideas and have discussions on different subjects. One good idea shared with another good idea becomes two better ideas when exchanged. Change is inevitable and it cannot be avoided; hence, we should adapt ourselves accordingly and conduct ourselves as positively and creatively as possible.
7. Man is the master of his fate. He can shape his destiny according to his own imagination. Use your imagination in such a way that your tough and unfamiliar path of life gets illuminated.
8. Keep your mind alert. Use it to probe, examine, and analyse situations to obtain a positive solution. Promote positive attitude in all walks of life.
9. Do something that others cannot do. Think of something different that others cannot think of.
10. Try to find and examine the success methods that successful people have used in their journeys up the

ladder and then adopt and adapt those methods to fit your own style.

11. Suggest a solution along with your complaint.
12. Meditate to enhance your creative abilities.
13. Understand other's thoughts deeply. This will widen your scope of thinking and will indicate a new path in your thought process.
14. Always try to invent new ideas. Never hesitate to experiment with ideas and situations. In most cases new ideas and new experiments lead to some new invention.
15. Do any work in your own unique and positive way.
16. Develop the curiosity to know and learn about new things and subjects.
17. Try and be in the company of those people who are creative.
18. It's easy to walk on the beaten path. Try to create your own new path.
19. When some new ideas strike, write them down and in time act upon them.

We remain happy and content in the same place and in the same position where we are. We do not develop the courage to move forward in a new direction and do better for ourselves. We pass our entire lives believing in the formula – "At least work is going on." But why? Why can't we become better and bolder?

Group Discussions

To develop and encourage creative thinking and exchange new ideas, group discussions are a useful practice. Here are some pointers on how to carry out a successful group discussion:

1. Motivate every member to participate.
2. Prevent domination by any one individual.
3. Stimulate discussions with appropriate questions.
4. Control extent of diversion from main topic.
5. Use additional means, such as audio, video, paper, board, etc., wherever necessary.
6. Make a clear plan of the discussion and keep a track of time.
7. Ask related questions to take the discussion forward.
8. Summarise each topic at the end.
9. Avoid heated arguments.
10. Translate unclear statements made by any member.
11. If there is any disagreement at any time, then repeat to bring back pleasantness into the discussion.
12. Make the discussion fruitful.
13. Complete the incomplete statements made by members.
14. Move to the next topic at an appropriate time.

The Power of Praise

Praise and admiration touch our heart. It makes us happy. It nourishes our soul in the same way as food and water nourish our body.

A person who often praises is dear to us.

A praise that mentions someone's positive qualities is genuine praise. The motive of such praise is to motivate the receiver to continue and further improve his qualities. If one is not praised for his goodness, bravery and other such qualities then these traits lose their importance and ultimately diminish. Hence, the positive qualities of a person must definitely be praised.

There is another type of praise that is aimed at boosting self-confidence of a weak-minded person by praising him for his qualities. Praise and appreciation improve and strengthen his inner strength and concentration.

Individuals possessing the skill and expertise in the art of praising know how to get their work done, and are also able to maintain co-ordination with anyone.

Exaggerated praise is called flattery. This is done by individuals to further their own interests.

Most people fall prey to flattery and prefer to get ruined by it rather than improving themselves from constructive criticism.

Praising and appreciating someone for possessing good qualities and values in life, or good principles and habits such as, truthfulness, virtuousness, honesty, etc., leads to improving and enhancing an individual's character.

Personality Development

It is not important for a person to be a celebrity or an officer at a high post to possess a good personality. One can have an attractive personality at any grade in life. A person with good qualities can command respect anywhere. A person should develop good qualities by self-analysis. The following are some pointers:

1. Whatever you do perform it with your full ability.
2. Be self-motivated.
3. Be a good listener.
4. Work with devotion.
5. Be calm and humble.
6. Have a praising nature.
7. Be fearless and bold.
8. Always be happy.
9. Always be friendly.
10. Be self-confident.
11. Be active to please anybody.
12. Have common sense.
13. Be impressive.
14. Keep a positive attitude.
15. Become special from ordinary.

First Impression

Whenever we meet a person, the first impression that we create should be the best. To achieve this:

1. Keep smiling and listen carefully to others.
2. Always keep your face towards the person to whom you are talking to if you are standing.
3. Ask questions from people and try to know about their opinion. In addition to facts, try to understand their ideas and feelings.
4. Always praise others. By doing this you will win their faith and belief.
5. Meet people and try to find out the common interests that you share with them.
6. Share jokes with people. By laughing together, people become friends easily.
7. To avoid hesitation, talk to other people by taking the initiative yourself.
8. Speak in a voice level that can be heard without straining.
9. When you first meet a person, focus on positive comments rather than criticism and complaints.
10. Discuss various topics while conversing and always talk in the interest of the other person. By doing so, friendship becomes easier.
11. Try and discuss on everyday-life topics. Common topics should be discussed rather than personal topics.

12. Tell the other person about your passions and interests and try to know about theirs. Try and be charming when you meet someone for the first time, because people set their mind on the basis of the first meeting.

One's real appearance reflects the good qualities that one possesses. The impression created too should be of good qualities and not that of a good appearance.

The Ability To Adjust

Circumstances and situations in life keep changing. None of us are aware of what the future holds for us and what unfortunate and unimaginable things may happen. To battle life's storm and sail through unhurt, one should have the tendency to change according to situation, mould the situation into a favourable one or to completely surrender. Try to develop an attitude of adjustment in life.

Sometimes we become impatient at the thought of the other person not paying attention to us; he neither surrenders nor is ready to adapt according to the situation. Hence, it makes sense to change oneself ahead of time.

When we become friendly, then the other person also becomes friendly or comfortable with us.

Sometimes the nature and ideas of people living a family or otherwise collide with each other; this results in quarrels and the atmosphere becomes disturbed. To tackle such problems and conflicts, individuals should have the capability to change themselves or to bow themselves or be friendly with each other, only then can they continue to exist peacefully with one another.

Even two people living together for a long time get impatient with each other. They start fighting on petty issues that sometimes do not even concern them.

By being practical and reasonable one can learn to compromise and live harmoniously with others before time passes them by. By doing this we can lead a peaceful life.

During a storm, the big trees tend to fall because they cannot bow themselves in the direction of the strong winds, but the small bushes do not collapse because they bow in the direction of the wind and weather the storm.

An adverse situation in one's life is so much like a storm. Those people who adjust themselves according to situations and surrender to time, are easily able to confront life's obstacles and sufferings.

The Power of Love

Love is another name of humanity. The ultimate mystery of life, religion, and action lies in love. Without love, one cannot understand the essential truth of life. Love for God, love for one another, love for animals, love for the country, are all sentiments that exist as a result of love being in each one of us. Love is an action. Whenever you extend your hands to help others, your legs too move ahead to help the poor and needy. Your eyes start seeing their trouble and your ears start listening to their plight; then you start loving them.

Love is not to take but to give. It is a synonym for giving, not accepting. The process of give and take is not called love but is termed business.

Love is the greatest doctor. When you learn to love completely, you do not require any medicine.

Love can solve any kind of problems.

Love is the only true magnet that can attract any person in this world.

A person who loves is truly happy and lucky. Love eliminates fatigue. It turns all pain into pleasure. The entire world seems beautiful if there is love in one's heart.

Love in relationships increases only when we do not have the desire to take but to give the maximum to the person whom we love.

Whatever be the kind of relation, expression of love keeps it alive. You may be tied in any kind of relationship, be it husband–wife or brother–sister or mother–child, if you give a compliment from the depth of your heart, then the other person will be full of love for you and there will be a wonderful feeling of pleasure in the relationship.

Expressing love is very important. It is essential that the other person know your feelings and emotions. The foundation of love is expression.

For maintaining close relations, it is not necessary to constantly express your love by saying "I love you;" what is important is to talk in your partner's style.

Use your special talents and ideas to express your love for someone special. A beautiful painting or a good poem is more effective in representing love than an expensive gift.

If somebody helps you in situations that are out of their limit, then it should be accepted that this person loves you and will always help you in any situation.

If your companion presents to you such type of gifts that are useful to you, then it should be understood that he cares for you and thinks about your feelings more than his own. This type of a person will prove to be your best companion.

You do not love a woman because she is beautiful. She looks beautiful only because you love her.

In our day-to-day life we come across people who harass and torture others for their own benefit. This happens both at home and at work. To make life full of pleasure and happiness it is necessary that we should learn to use things and love people instead of using people and loving things.

If you cannot love the person who is visible and is with you, then how can you love someone you have never seen.

Do not hope for others to love you and give you attention. Instead you should love others and take care of them.

The biggest gift of loving somebody is to give them quality time.

If you want to be happy in your life then always love your work positively.

Do not love so much that their love becomes your weakness, but love so much that your love becomes someone's need.

Friendship

Humans have a natural tendency of making friends. Every person is in search of a true companion, a true friend, to whom he can talk open heartedly and can share his secrets of joy and sorrow.

The natural desire and need to have someone who can be your support system in good and bad phases of life is paramount. Someone, who can understand your feelings correctly and have sympathy for you.

Such a relation of friendship creates an atmosphere of trust where one can share the expression of his internal and external life without any hesitation.

It is impossible that difficult situations will not arise in one's life. Troubles can come to anyone at anytime, be it rich or poor, strong or weak. Sometimes the difficulties are so unexpected and complicated that it becomes almost impossible to handle them suddenly. At that time, true friends are required who can help you survive in difficult situations.

With the co-operation of friends, life can be very easy, charming, and safe. Without friends, life becomes very lonely, deserted, and terrifying. A person who has a true friend has everything that is necessary and required in the way of life.

We usually see that very rich people who have a lot of money or power, are always surrounded with a lot of friends. But in this surrounding crowd, there is rarely a true friend. Most of these people float around and keep company only for greed. Once their motive is over, they tend to take their own way and disappear.

Friendship cannot be attained on the basis of money, and it is true that money is responsible for making enemies by creating greed, jealousy, and hatred among people.

Your best friend is one who does not share your weaknesses with others but tells you about them to your face.

In friendship, love is above all and love has no selfishness at all. It is human behaviour that can make someone a friend or an enemy.

It is natural and easy to make friends with people who are naturally gentle, are calm, and are good in nature; action, and character.

Those persons who have lived false, disorganised and a declining life, and who even now have not made their mind and conduct believable, are not considered suitable for friendship. Such people, even if they give confidence or take an oath, are usually not considered safe for friendship.

The life of a person becomes frightening, annoying, full of harm and grief, if he is surrounded by obscene, imprudent, treacherous, debased, and inferior friends.

Although friendship is necessary in this world, it is difficult to find a true and sincere friend. So it is better to have a few number of friends who are true, than to have tons of them who are selfish and mean.

Having fake friends is more dangerous than having enemies. The blow caused by an enemy may be evaded, but the blow caused by a fake friend never fails.

It may not be possible for you to make a list of five friends, but for others try to be on their list as one of their five close friends.

Do not love a friend who insults you but never insult a friend who loves you.

Even the best of friends will leave your company when commitments are not fulfilled.

The best way to get rid of enemies is to make them your friends.

Consider your spouse, children, family members, and other relatives first as your friends and then family and try and develop close relations with them. Be their true friend and make them your true friend with sincerity and nobility.

Your inner conscience is your best friend; always listen to it.

Other friends:

Friend	in foreign	Education
Friend	in trouble	Patience
Friend	at residence	Spouse
Friend	in sickness	Doctor
Friend	for economic security	Life insurance advisor
Friend	for conduct	Knowledge
Friend	for war	Courage
Friend	to march ahead	Confidence
Friend	in old age	Money
Friend	at death	Religion

Give ample opportunities to your enemy to become your friend,
but
do not give any opportunity to your friend to become your enemy.

Mental Block

A state of mental block is when the mind tells us that we are incapable or inept at a particular task, whereas our sensibilities tell us that we are capable enough to complete that work.

Whenever an elephant is captured for the first time, it is tied by strong chains to a big tree. For some days it tries hard to free himself but fails. In the end, it gives up and accepts the situation. Later, even when it is tied by a weak chain to a small tree, it does not try to fight back as the perception in its mind is that it cannot break free. This is an example of a mental block.

"I cannot do this work, it is not possible for me" and some of the different kinds of mental locks that have a hold in our mind.

A negative attitude is a big companion of mental block. Because of this state of mental block, we are unable to do many positive things and hence are unable to give up our bad habits. By developing a positive mind set, we can remove this mental block from our minds.

Always remember, nothing is impossible in this world.

Once we pledge that we will go ahead and remove our mental block, then no goal will be unthinkable for us.

Without effort, nature will not allow you to proceed further.

Superstition (Blind Faith)

Any belief based on fear or ignorance is called superstition or blind faith.

Blind faith does not have any solid foundation. It develops its deep roots on the basis of illusion or coincidence or imagination.

The manner of our upbringing, our longing for material things, and the fear in our minds about certain things gives birth to superstitions in our life. We are deeply influenced by the surroundings in which we grow and are brought up. It is natural for a child to become religious and superstitious, if the environment under which he was brought up was under the influence of religion and blind faith. It is natural tendency for a child to believe in what his elders tell him. In most cases the elders are superstitious, and they fill a child's mind with unrealistic and irrational thoughts, thereby affecting the child with innumerable superstitions and false beliefs. This process of influencing the younger generation continues and with time becomes a vicious cycle. Such children grow up to be confused and lack self-confidence. They depend on others to make decisions for them live a life enslaved by false beliefs and opinions. In our society, different people have different beliefs, different superstitions, and different rituals that they follow. When a group of people begin believing in any of these, it gives birth to a new religious community. Such people and communities, even though they commit crimes, come to be believed and accepted by the masses as being religious and spiritual.

Some people under the cover of belief and superstition try to escape from the responsibility of their mistakes.

Unscrupulous and fraudulent people take advantage of people with false beliefs and cheat them.

People who are afraid of facing reality and who have a sense of insecurity about themselves are the ones who get caught in the trap of superstitions. The fear of the evil gives rise to different fears in their minds which becomes the base of all their superstitions.

We may have made materialistic progress and may also claim to exist in a literate and civilised society, but mentally we are still restricted by countless superstitions. The expanse of false beliefs in our lives is so vast that even with the emergence of new thought systems we are not able to entirely free ourselves from the grasp of superstitions. These deep-rooted beliefs in our family systems and traditions are handed down from one generation to the next. Even the learned in our society have so many superstitious, conservative, and traditional people who continue to remain in the dark world of false beliefs and even fall prey to frauds and hypocrites.

People who are under the clutches of superstitions put up fetters for themselves in their lives, and they unnecessarily restrain their freedom of expression or action. They suffer from low self-confidence because the credit of their success or failure is always based on a specific day, thing, or any matter that does not have any base or logic. The tradition of lighting a lamp was to illuminate the darkness; it had nothing to do with rituals.

Another superstition that exists in North India is the act of gambling on *Diwali* night, which is considered auspicious. History is evident that gambling not only impairs family life but has also made people bankrupt.

The act of gambling leads to increased greed resulting in loss of property, possessions, and wealth. Being dependent on superstitions for every action and endeavour in life is a foolish and lazy way of trying to achieve one's means. For instance, if a person has no permanent means of livelihood, then he should attempt to first regularise his income by getting involved in some business or job. But if he remains unconcerned towards his means of livelihood, and continues to depend on false presumptions that maybe he will gain by placing a statue, fountain, plant, or some "magical" product inside or outside his house or office, then he is merely fooling himself and being irresponsible and reckless with his life as well as deceiving and denying his family their due. Such superstitious people can never be considered trustworthy or reliable.

Some of the superstitions that we notice in our daily lives actually have no importance or relevance to our work or lives but have become so strongly ingrained in our minds that we refuse to let go of them. Some such superstitions, such as the act of sneezing when going for some important work, black cat crossing the way, someone calling from behind while moving out for work, seeing an empty or filled vessel coming from front, still exist today. On the basis of these superstitions people try to decide in advance the result of their approaching failure or success and end up postponing their work which leads to unnecessary losses and delays.

Remember, there is no wrong time to do a right work.

Believing in superstitions strengthens our faith in false beliefs and makes us weak, inefficient, and lazy. Superstitions become obstacles in our personal growth and also prevent a community as a whole from developing and advancing. People especially from the backward classes are known to be very involved in such practices – magical arts, incantations, witchcraft, influence of the evil eye, etc. The negative results of all of these are known to us and their effects too are visible from time to time.

How can one get rid of superstitions permanently? For this, we first need to find the source of such superstitions; from where exactly do they originate? The root cause will almost always be greed and fear.

Once people are able to realise that the effect of superstitions cannot be sustained, gradually superstitions will start fading away. Their short life span will destroy them completely from the root.

Though we are all free to adopt whichever way of thinking suits us, but our thoughts should be scientific and logical and should take us forward in life. Scientific and logical thinking means decisions are made only after proper and logical reasoning and that the thinking is free from all kinds of superstitions and false beliefs. Scientific and logical thinking increases one's self-confidence and such people do not fall prey to imposters who pose as well wishers and involve us in false beliefs. Mentally strong and determined people control their mind, actions, and their life and avoid being carried away by shortcuts offered by useless superstitions that promise almost everything. They never get cheated by frauds and hypocrites because they control their lives by their own logical decisions and not by the so-called "agents of invisible powers".

On the other hand, people who are under the influence of superstitions are continuously cheated in the name of religion by frauds and hypocrites, who offer false and bogus alternatives and make these weak people their slaves. Gradually with time people become so dependent on these godmen that they lose their sense of discrimination and begin to be completely governed by these religious imposters. A positive and good living can be achieved only if we refuse to fall prey to superstitions or any false beliefs that not only make us irresponsible towards our duties in life but also force us to live a life of a slave. Today, it is the duty of every responsible citizen to firmly oppose the stronghold of these superstitions in our society so that the future generations are free from the harmful effects of these false beliefs as well as from the influence of tricksters.

Depression

Depression is the biggest problem being faced by us these days. It leads to a break in relations; suicide cases have also increased due to depression.

This is a psychological disorder that is caused as a result of the various complications of modern life. A depressed person begins to believe that he is ill even though he has no signs of any disease. He continues to change his clinicians in search of one who can diagnose some illness in him. Such patients suffer from negative emotions that lead to a rapidly reducing resistance power (low immunity). The patient has a feeling of despair, insecurity, and hopelessness. These people do not like to make friends, meet, or talk to anyone.

Symptoms

1. Constantly seem to be surrounded by sadness and a feeling of restlessness; remain in a contaminated mood due to some reason or the other.
2. Have no expectation from life; suffer from great disappointment.
3. Constant feeling of guilt. Life seems a burden. Feel helpless at all times; not able to do the chosen work.
4. Have no interest in their favourite activities.
5. Have a constant feeling of decreased energy levels, and the body feels extremely tired even after light activity.
6. Suffer from sleeping problems; may wake up early or may continue to sleep for extremely long hours.
7. May either experience loss of weight due to a poor appetite, or may get obese by overeating.

8. May have a feeling to commit suicide or may even attempt to commit suicide.

Causes and Prevention

If we try and analyse our behaviour and attitude, we will find that not only is the cause of depression within us, its prevention is also with us.

We always try to find reasons for our troubles outside and hence find faults with others and hold them responsible for our own discomforts. We forever blame others, while we ourselves are the cause of our own worries and anxieties. We forever hold others responsible for our own failures, disappointments, anger, estranged relations, misfortunes, etc. Identify your mistakes, accept them, and control yourself. It is human inclination to blame others and hold them responsible for their own wrong deeds. Every individual, no matter how much he shifts blame to others, is accountable for his problems and sufferings. The sooner each one of us realises this, the faster we will be able to solve our problems and prevent ourselves from suffering from depression.

None of us want to change ourselves. We are forever trying to change others as per our wishes and wants. This approach of ours is the sole reason for the majority of problems in our lives. We expect the other person to change, and think that once this happens our problems will get solved automatically and our sorrows will change into happiness.

Humans are very strange. They tend to forget that if they cannot change themselves according to others' wishes, how can they then expect others to change? If this simple fact is understood by all of us, more than half the time and energy that we waste to change others can be used to change ourselves and be truly happy.

A sad person always has one thing on his mind – "I am the only sad person and everybody around is happy". It is his belief that all the sad moments are destined for him only. He feels that the sadness of others is much less in comparison to the sadness he suffers from. He thinks his problems are unique and different, and that what he is going through and tolerating nobody else can. Such a thought process and belief about his sadness, makes him even more sad and depressed.

Count your sorrows the same way you count your happiness. Consider how fortunate you are in the following manner – if I am able to see with my eyes, then I am luckier than the large number of visually handicapped people around us; if I am able to hear, then I am better than the vast number of hearing impaired persons; if I can read and write, then I am much more fortunate than the millions who are illiterate or have not had the opportunity to go to school; if I have food on my plate, clothing to cover me, and my own house to provide me shelter, then I am richer than 75% of the population in this world. Once you write such types of things down up to a count of 50, you will realise for yourselves what a blessed state you are in. Thus, it is all in the perception of things and in how we perceive situations.

We know that one day all happiness becomes sorrow and so does sorrow transform to happiness. Night is never constant; morning always follows. No matter how big or strong a storm, stillness always comes next.

Without sorrow, happiness cannot be realised.

Do not become dejected by comparing your life with others. Believe in the fact that you are the most unique and special person in this world. There is no other person in this world as you.

Disorders caused by depression can be cured by both naturopathy and yoga. The more you consume a natural diet, the more you will benefit. It is very beneficial to practice *Trataka* to handle depression.

A person suffering from depression should get a minimum of seven hours of sleep every day. Lack of sufficient sleep can increase depression. Also, being busy and occupied in activities helps heal depression. Regular counselling sessions with friends or a professional psychologist with whom one is comfortable sharing and discussing problems help. During such sessions all information shared should be kept confidential, and the patient should not be criticised for any of his actions or thoughts. Such sessions generate confidence in the sufferer, and he is able to handle his problems calmly and positively. In the case of children, parents should also be involved in the counselling sessions along with the child.

Work and Destiny

We shape our destiny by the work we do. This work results in our destiny or fate. Thus, humans are the creators of their destiny. We create our destiny according to the work we do. A lazy person blames his destiny, but an active and dutiful individual treats it as his deed and works hard towards it. Nature decides when and in which birth the result of our actions will be rewarded.

It is according to the fruits of one's deeds that someone takes birth in a well-to-do family while someone is born underprivileged. Two children take birth in the same place, in the same atmosphere but both the children are different. This is a result of their individual actions over several cycles of births. The cycle of birth and death has continued since ages, and the deeds and fruits of our actions cannot be evaluated in a single birth. These have got collected over eons of time. Why is one person happy and other suffering? Why is one person pleased and wealthy while the other is dejected and poor? Why does one person have good health and intelligence but the other has sufferings and illnesses? We need to ponder on such questions. What has made us land in the situation that we are in, are points that we need to reflect on.

Today whichever situation we are in, good or bad, is a result of our past deeds. What we will be tomorrow depends on the good or bad deeds that we do today. Hence, a person can make or break his own destiny. His destiny is in his hands. Fortune or misfortune, it is all the result of his deeds.

One person is mentally slow and has a slow memory, while the other person is intelligent and has a sharp memory. This is knowledge-related destiny.

Any person who creates obstacles for others to obtain knowledge truly insults scholars, disregards intellect, and earns a knowledge-related misfortune for himself. But a person who helps in the education of others, trains people, and respects intelligence, creates knowledge-related fortune for himself.

One person is healthy and rarely becomes sick, is physically strong and does not get tired by laborious activity. Another person mostly remains ill with various medical conditions such as heart disease, diabetes, thyroid problems, abdominal complaints, etc. This is called health-related destiny.

A person who troubles others causing agitation and harassment faces health-related misfortunes. In harming others he causes harm to himself and this takes a toll on his health. But, a person who does not trouble others and lives a nonviolent and friendly life, in fact creates health-related fortunes for himself.

One person gets recognition and people respect his word. Another person is disgraced and is not able to become a favourite with the people. This is reputation-related destiny.

A person who proudly, criticises others, behaves arrogantly, creates reputation-related misfortunes. A person who is not proud and prudish, but praises others and behaves with nobility, creates reputation-related fortunes.

One person normally remains calm and humble and lives a simple and easy life. Another person is very disturbed, is always in a state of frenzy on the smallest of issues and abuses others in anger. This is emotion-related destiny.

A person with negative thoughts creates an emotion-related misfortunes and a person with positive thoughts creates emotion-related fortunes.

Therefore, a person who has deceived others will earn himself treacherous (faithless) associates. But, the person who does good to others gets trustworthy (faithful) associates.

The truth is that it is we humans who are solely responsible for our own fortunes or misfortunes.

In our daily lives we come across several individuals who are virtuous and righteous but seem to be going through hardships in their lives. And then we see individuals who employ unfair means and commit sins, but seem to be enjoying their lives with pleasure and happiness. Such circumstances create doubts in our minds and we begin to doubt God and his decisions. What we fail to understand is that we all bear the fruits of our own actions. So, the virtuous person who seems to be troubled in his present life is not suffering due to his present actions but due to his actions of the past. Similarly, the sinful person who seems to be enjoying the best in his present life is enjoying the fruits of his past deeds and is not successful due to his present immoral and corrupt actions. There is enough evidence in history to show that all great kings, rulers, scholars, sages, and brave and strong warriors at one time in their lives became helpless and had to bear the consequences of their actions, good or bad.

Leading a righteous and principled life includes earning one's living in an ethical manner. If you earn money using wrong sources or gain from unethical profits, then this money earned by unfair means will not bear positive fruits for you or for your family, and you may all have to suffer. You may experience the following:

1. Medical problems in the house; a family member may come down with some chronic or prolonged illness.
2. Huge losses.
3. Early death of a family member that may distress you throughout your life.
4. Divorce of a son or daughter or of self.
5. You or a family member may lead a life of a vagrant.
6. Negligence towards parents by their young children.
7. Due to circumstances beyond control, children living separately from their aged parents.
8. One or more person in the family being aggressive and having an angry disposition.

9. Difference of opinion in the family.
10. Become a victim of conspiracy causing loss of prestige, life, property, etc.
11. Disability by birth or accident of a family member or of self.

Good actions never go wasted. No one can deny you the money, fame, prosperity that is in your destiny and to which you are entitled. So, then why indulge in corrupt and immoral means to earn a living?

Some people earn a lot of money owing to their destiny but they can't use it. This may be because they are too ill to enjoy it. Some people are unable to earn a lot of money but do not have a dearth of anything in their lives. Then there are some people who have both the destiny to get the money as well as the destiny to use it. The fruits of our actions come in the form of the varied circumstances we go though in life. Favourable situations are the result of our good deeds and adverse situations are the result of our bad deeds. So, it is foolish to be happy or sad in such situations. As humans we are capable of using our sense of discrimination, unlike animals who merely bear the fruits of their actions. It is only humans who have the power to correct their past misdeeds by generating good and positive deeds in their present birth. No action is impossible; it may seem difficult at first but we can succeed if we put in all our positive efforts and try. We can make our own destiny with our hard work.

Destiny is shaped by hard work

Most people keep complaining about the unfavourable circumstances they are in and continue to expect that circumstances will become favourable and they will then succeed. But, what they do not realise is that circumstances cannot be favourable at all times in life. Life is full of ups and downs and it has to be lived bravely, displaying a lot of courage to reach the peak of success. Courageous and hard working people do not wait for circumstances to turn in their favour, instead with hard work they make the circumstances turn in their favour. When we succeed, we accept our success as divine blessing; but it is in fact our own hard work and discipline, and of course God's blessings, that sees us through. If we have worked hard our success should not surprise us, because there is no alternative to hard work.

The Art of Learning

Learning is a process that continues throughout one's life. Knowledge is profitable than money. We use external security guards to keep our money safe from thieves, but knowledge gives us lifelong security.

From knowledge we gain respect, finance, high position, and dignity in the society.

Knowledge is not granted; it is gained. We cannot transfer knowledge but can surely accumulate it throughout our lives. If knowledge could be given then the Pandavas and Kauravas would have been archers and not Eklavya. Any person with the continuous craving for knowledge will always find a chance to learn.

Learning in one's life can happen from anywhere – from books, through people, from television, by attending special courses, etc. One can learn through reading, listening, watching, thinking, or even by practically carrying out certain activities. We normally tend to forget what we hear, we understand what we see, but we always remember what we do.

Learning can also occur from failures.

Always learn through mistakes – from your own as well as from others. A person who learns from others' mistakes is wise, whereas the person who learns from his own mistakes is ordinary. The person who does not learn from mistakes is a fool.

Learn new things according to your needs. The biggest need is the learning of behavioural knowledge. A person who collects money and does not use it is as big a fool as a person who gains knowledge but does not put it to use.

A person who stops learning is considered to be old aged.-It does not matter whether the age is 20 or 80 years. And the person who continues to learn remains young forever.

Importance of Books

Reading books inspires individuals to form good habits and awakens and excites the mind to learn more. The habit of reading books helps one realize their mistakes and helps one find solutions to shortcomings in their conduct. Books serve as instructors through which one gets guidance, peace of mind, and happiness.

There is unlimited knowledge stored in books. There is no friend like knowledge and no enemy like ignorance. Knowledge assists youngsters to live within boundaries, is a support in old age, and is a source of income when used professionally.

One can enjoy its company just as that of wise scholars.

Reading books is the cheapest way of entertainment and the enjoyment is long lasting.

Books that stimulate the mind and intellect are the best self-help books one can read. While reading such books, make it a point to highlight certain sections or sentences in the book that interest you, so that you can get back to them at leisure.

Good books are our faithful friends but bad books are our worst enemies.

Anger Management

Anger is a natural emotion which is ventilated due to frustration, disappointment, aggressiveness, and sometimes failure. A bout of anger can range from slight irritation to a high loss of temper.

Anger is a mixture of bad thoughts, which includes enmity, sadness, fear, insult, ego, and indiscretion.

Different Types of Anger

Anger can be divided into two categories – passive anger (suppressed anger) and aggressive anger (forceful anger).

Passive anger

If the following typical features are present, a person is characterized as having passive anger.

- Criticizing someone behind his back, avoiding eye contact, and trying to insult others.
- Provoking others by spreading negative ideas and thoughts, while keeping yourself safe on the other side. Thinking of yourself as being guilty at all times and asking for pardoning without any reason.
- Losing one's anger on needless things and situations while ignoring important things.
- Suffering from obsessive compulsive disorder (becoming more concerned about things such as cleaning and washing, double checking things, having illogical feelings about small and worthless things).
- Avoiding solving one's problems and running away from quarrels to avoid situations that lead to debates and arguments.

Aggressive anger

The following features suggest a person suffers from aggressive anger.

- Threatening others, passing ironical remarks, striking with the fist or beating up others, or honking loudly when in traffic.
- Physically attacking others, name calling, not caring about others' emotions, and punishing others for no fault of theirs.
- Breaking and damaging objects, throwing temper tantrums, hurting animals, ruining a relationship between two people, driving recklessly, shouting loudly, and blaming others for one's own mistakes.
- Speaking quickly, overworking, and expecting others to work in the same way.
- Showing off, seeking people's attention at all times, ignoring the needs of others, and crossing the limits in most situations.
- Remembering the unfortunate moments of the past at all times and not being able to forgive others.

Disadvantages of Anger

Anger is said to be the biggest enemy of health. It can also be called momentary madness when anger strikes wrong decisions are made that lead to unfortunate situations. Anger makes people suffer from digestive problems, mental troubles, heart-related disorders, and many such health problems. The muscular system too loses its strength and ability to work. Anger gives rise to ailments such as high blood pressure (hypertension), diabetes, heart attacks, paralysis, and at times cancer too. The mind too gets affected when excessive anger is present. It suffers from emotions such as sadness, restlessness, and tension.

To get angry is like stabbing one's body with a knife.

A person may not get tired of working from morning till evening, but the feeling of anger can tire a person in only an hour. Getting angry is like giving punishment to yourself for the wrong deeds of others.

An angry person can neither be a warrior nor a good player. He would never be successful in the field of competition.

Anger ruins lives. The person to whom anger is shown becomes displeased, relations break down, and quarrels take place. The presence of anger makes personal, family, and social life very unpleasant and at times destructive.

Episodes of anger are responsible for developing differences in husband-wife relationships, father-son relations, as well as disagreements between brothers, sisters, and other such family relations.

Anger is the root cause of many crimes around the world. Fights, murders, suicides, and many such brutal acts take place under the influence of anger. Anger casts a shadow on an individual's mind and clouds the thoughts and power of reasoning, and this is what leads to barbaric acts of cruelty in a civilized society. Anger at times results in such harmful actions that its compensation is impossible or extremely difficult.

Anger has an adverse effect on the upbringing of young children. Children of angry parents become either introverts or are extremely aggressive.

Anger is similar to a mental storm; when it comes it destroys the patience and tolerance of an individual. Anger is a mental illness that does not give a chance to thinking, consideration, and understanding.

Anything said in anger leaves a permanent sign, such as a mark left behind from the driving of a nail in wood. Anger pierces the heart and mind and remains there permanently.

Anger usually starts with foolishness and ends on repentance. A person who has a decreased tolerance level will get angry more often

Anger destroys a person's auspicious actions, positive feelings, and good qualities in the same way as a flood destroys a beautiful garden.

Note: Scolding or carrying out an act of artificial anger does not harm anyone, particularly if you immediately become normal.

Causes of Anger

Damage of some kind in our work or some deficiency in it, some other problem or obstacle, incomplete expectations, not getting early results, unexpected results, standing in a long queue, stuck in a traffic jam, some work not completed in the stipulated time result in an increase in restlessness and uneasiness, which then become the cause of anger.

- If you are disorganised, undisciplined, overloaded by work and are in stress then you will get more angry.
- If someone hurts our sentiments by any means then too we become angry.
- A long confused situation may be the result of anger.
- Anger comes when a senior or boss scolds.
- A low tolerance level causes anger.
- Some persons develop a habit of getting angry as a result of their other family members being angry.
- Anger also happens when one is in a state of fear, guilt, or despair.
- Being cheated may make a person angry and aggressive.
- Insufficient sleep or insomnia can cause a person to become irritated and angry.
- Anger may also result when the needs of the family members are not met.

- Children retain anger in their minds if they do not receive love and affection from their parents and after growing up the suppressed anger is released.

How To Overcome Anger

There are three ways to overcome anger.

1. *Before getting angry:*

- Try to find your own fault before blaming others.
- Adopting a positive attitude helps eliminate negative thinking.
- You cannot change others but you can change yourself.
- Whatever cannot be changed should be accepted happily.
- Convince yourself that restlessness and hurry result in waste. Every job takes its own time. Do not get excited by hearing only one side of the story. Make your decision only after you have heard both the sides.
- Do not force the new generation to think and behave like it was in your own generation.
- Do not see *who* is wrong but try to see *what* is wrong.
- Whatever the consequence, accept it happily; know that whatever God does is for the best.
- A happy and cheerful person can control anger easily.
- Always be ready to accept change, because change is the rule of nature.
- Learn to forgive. For a happy future enmity should be converted into friendship.
- By consuming pure (*satvik*) food anger can be controlled.
- Make an effort to regularly read such literature that leads to physical, mental, and spiritual development.

- As you expect from others, do the same to them.
- Do not hope for expectations from others. Any good deed done for them will not go to waste; it will come back some time in the form of some rewards.
- If another person is angry, then the wise thing to do is remain silent and only listen to him.
- A tolerant person always wins. Try to stay away from those people who make you angry.

2. ***When you are angry:***

- Whenever you expect a situation that will make you angry, always drink a glass of water and try to change the topic.
- When you are angry, give a chance to others to speak. If the other person is accepting his mistake then give him a chance and try and control your anger.
- Remember, when an enemy makes you angry it is to reduce your energy or he is trying to extort your secrets.
- It is harmful to get excited by any action and give a reaction immediately.
- Whenever you are angry think about its consequences.
- Think, will everything be fine by getting angry. Before getting angry, consider the physical, mental, and family situation of the other person.
- Never ignore the age of the person on whom you are losing your temper. If it is a child, give him a chance to improve. If it is an older person, then take care of his respect.
- Teach and explain the other person how to work instead of getting irritated with him. Always give a clear and precise reason to the person with whom you are angry.

- Speak out your mental agony peacefully.
- Learn to disagree without anger.
- If the other person is angry always try to talk to him in a peaceful manner. Try to tell him that the differences can be solved by regular meetings and discussions.
- Remaining silent helps greatly in controlling anger.
- If experiencing extreme anger, massage your ears.
- If the atmosphere of anger is not conducive for a debate, then either leave the place for some time or change the topic of conversation.
- If the policy of "One said and the other accepted; people say both are wise", is adopted by us in our everyday lives not only will anger be reduced, we will also live lesser stressful lives.

3. ***After getting angry:***

- You can reduce your anger and come out of it by saying "sorry" to the person with whom you were angry; this can be done without considering who he is and what is his position.
- Control your anger by putting yourself in the other person's shoes and thinking what would you have done if you were in his position.
- Do not take any sudden decisions when you are in anger.
- Write down in detail what is the cause of your anger and how you think it can be reduced.
- When angry go for a walk to some park, to the bank of a river, or to some beach. It is easy to control anger in a calm and peaceful atmosphere.
- Anger can also be controlled by listening to the music of your choice.

- On getting angry, make a punching bag or take a pillow and express your anger by continuously punching it. This not only releases your anger, but also helps burn wasteful energy that is stored in the body.
- Engage yourself in some activity that interests you so that anger is reduced quickly such as brisk walking, dancing, watering plants, etc.
- Laugh and take a deep breath.
- Splash some cold water on your face when angry.
- Try and reason – is it correct that we burn the fire of anger within us because other people who make mistakes?
- Always discard anger before going to bed. Before sleeping be silent for some time; if possible meditate and do a self-analysis.
- We normally blame others for making us angry. But this only means that you have given the strings of your life in the hands of somebody else. He may please you or upset you whenever he wants.
- You should say "I got angry" instead of saying "he made me angry". It means that you are in control of yourself and are not being controlled by somebody else.
- When the wordings, "I am the centre of my life" get stronger in the mind only then can we keep ourselves calm.
- It is our wrong deeds, our luck, and our destiny that are a cause of our pain or troubles.
- If the other person is only an excuse then why should we get angry?

Power of Anger

- If we suppress anger then the anger within will destroy us.
- If we express anger then it will damage our relationships.
- Therefore, we can control the power of anger and conquer it; once this happens, anger can be diverted for use in creative and meaningful activities.

If the power of anger is used in the right direction then one not only gets health, happiness, and success but also gets name and fame. There are numerous examples of various personalities who got immense success by using their power of anger in the proper manner. A few of those names are Mahatma Gandhi, Kalidas, Tulsidas, Chanakya, Dhruv, etc., who were especially notable.

A person who has conquered anger is a true warrior in the battlefield of life He is the master of all happiness, and his life becomes great.

Rectification of Mistakes

History proves that nobody has become great without making mistakes. The collection of mistakes over time is called experience; it takes one towards success.

To make a mistake is not bad but to not correct a mistake is bad. Hence, those people who inform us about our mistakes and give us the opportunity to correct them are our true friends. Never try to hold back from any action because there is a margin of error. Learn from the mistakes made, instead of trying to avoid oneself from making them. When you have made a mistake, realise it and try to understand your fault. Failure to understand and know your errors force you to repeat your mistakes and which in the long run proves to be harmful. To make a mistake is not such a serious offence, but what important is to learn from it and to not repeat it in the future.

A mistake that is not accepted or revealed gives birth to other different kinds of improper acts.

In many instances to hide our mistakes we make others responsible for our mistakes or most times we blame it on our destiny. Only when we take responsibility for our own actions can we improve upon them.

When pointing out mistakes made by others, instead of criticising them it is helpful if they can be told how to correct their mistakes so that they may not be repeated in future.

Treat the persons who make mistakes in the same way that you would like to be treated if you had made similar mistakes.

An intelligent person corrects his own mistakes by learning from the mistakes made by others.

Failure To Succeed

Failure is the first step on the ladder of success, because it is failure that shows one the way to the top of the ladder. Failure is an integral part of our lives. Success is not in never falling, but it is in to get up every time you fall.

Every child before taking a successful step or while learning to ride a bicycle, falls many times.

Adversity is our greatest teacher. We learn very less from our success. But we learn a lot from our failures.

Failure is the opportunity that you get to rise from your fall and begin again, this time more carefully and intelligently.

No success is stable; no failure is final. Hence never give up on your efforts to reach your goal.

Failure can have no existence in our lives until we believe in it completely and give in to it. This is when it begins to thrive in our lives and we become thorough failures. Failure does not mean one is weak or incapable.

It is those people who fail who think but do not do, and who do but do not think.

To improve on our failures we need to reconsider our shortcomings, our strengths and abilities, our attitude and viewpoint, as well as our optimism.

The most bankrupt person in the world is the one who has lost all enthusiasm in life; if in spite of losing all material possessions a person retains his enthusiasm, success will be his again.

Problems and Their Solutions

Problems are an integral part of our lives. Before we are able to solve one another problem arises. A challenge indeed but that's life.

Problems can come to any person at any time. Under unfortunate circumstances even a rich person can become poor.

If we study the lives of great men, we will find that their lives were full of hardships. Therefore, problems come to one and all, but what is important is how we handle them. Intelligent people treat obstacles in life as a challenge, but fools treat them as difficulties and get bogged down by them.

Problems and difficulties in life are similar to a lathe machine; they shape and shine our lives as well as our personalities. Every obstacle that we overcome builds our confidence and provides us encouragement to go on in life. Such a victory gives us immense satisfaction, which is an invaluable feeling that one can experience. Obstacles that stand in our way should not be viewed as difficulties, but as the rungs of the ladder of success.

Difficulties that we encounter in our lives strengthen our sense of judgement and encourage us to lead a fearless life. We all know that no matter what, we cannot shy away from problems in life; confronting them confidently and courageously helps us become stronger individuals.

Consider problems akin to a bag of cotton — big in size but light to lift. Use the hurdles of life to revive your hidden capabilities and brace yourself up for the challenges. All that is needed is a sensible head on the shoulders and a bit of courage to hang on. Armed with such an attitude, it is only a matter of time before problems start to disappear and we emerge stronger and better individuals.

Individuals who allow themselves to be overpowered by problems, suffer from distress and fear. Life becomes a burden and they are unable to think or act courageously. Their depressed attitude leads to newer kinds of problems and gradually from one single problem their problems develop into a mountain of obstacles. All that is simply needed is a bit of courage to handle this mountain of problems, but instead they bow down and accept defeat.

On the other hand a person who is determined to face challenges in life, does not care about the obstacles that stand in his way. His goal is to achieve success no matter what the hurdles.

Findings have shown that individuals who face obstacles in life right from the start are the ones who are successful and ultimately winners in life. One favourable way of tackling difficulties in life is to try and get to the root of the problem and then try and find a reason and a solution to it, because problems come with their own solution and they always bring a new opportunity with them, though at first they seem concealed.

Always be a part of the solution and not a part of the problem. Avoid going to your senior with a problem until you have found a solution to it. Encourage your juniors to come up with answers to the problems rather than merely expecting readymade solutions to them.

Optimists find opportunities in all difficulties, whereas pessimists find difficulties in all opportunities.

An obstacle that cannot be avoided should be seen as an opportunity to learn in life and one should know how to make the best use of them.

As an old adage goes: when the snake is alive, it eats the ants but when the snake is dead, the ants eat it. Times can change at any moment.

Always remember, when good days do not remain for always then the bad days too will not remain for long.

Weak people do not start any work due to the fear of problems arising. Erratic people start the work but leave it in the middle when some problem arises. Tough and strong people start the work and even while facing subsequent problems do not stop until the work they have undertaken is complete.

Intoxication Is A Curse

Intoxication of any substance is bad. It destroys an individual. Hence, it is very important to stay away from intoxication and if one does addicted then, he should try every possible method to get away from its clutch.

An addict can never be healthy or happy. Addiction is like cutting one's own feet with an axe.

Intoxication numbs the nerves and makes the addict sleepy. The brain becomes inactive. The tongue thickens, there is loss of taste, and the mouth does not open enough. The kidneys too get damaged. Episodes of cough and cold increase; and cavities fasten the process of loss of teeth. At a young age one feels old, and speech slows down.

Impotency too is caused by intoxicants. The nervous system including the sensory nerves becomes inactive. There is lack of vitality and the addict slowly and gradually surrenders moving on the path to self-destruction.

Family and social life also are affected by a life of addiction. Problems begin to brew within the family members and such disagreements then overflow into the society. This then is also the reason for the increasing crime rates in the society. Intoxicants are expensive. When the addict is not able to purchase his regular dose, he is pressured to procure it by unlawful means.

Tea/Coffee

Tea and coffee are the intoxicating products that civilised society enjoys. They destroy the resistance power of the body. Instead of consuming large amounts of tea or coffee, increased intake of tea prepared from basil, aniseed, or bran prove to be beneficial to the body. If these are not possible simply drink soup.

Pan Masala, Gutka, and Betel Nuts

These toxicants enter our body as our friends and destroy us by becoming our enemy.

Instead of chewing on *pan masala, gutka,* or betel nut take aniseed, cardamom, or chew *amla* (Indian gooseberry).

Smoking

Merely the curiosity to try smoking, to imitate their peers is causing our youth to take to smoking, which then in some time becomes an addiction. By the time they realise that it has become an addiction, it is too late; their lives are already covered by a blurred sheet of smoke. Every single cigarette smoked, consumes one page of the book called life. According to medical science and research, one cigarette turns seven minutes of our precious life to ashes. Some of the ill effects of smoking are:

- The chemical mixture of nicotine and carbon monoxide found in cigarettes swiftly increases the heart rate.
- Maximum ill effect of smoking is on the lungs; 95% of incidences of lung cancer are due to smoking.
- Many diseases of the digestive system arise as a result of smoking.
- The eyesight of smokers weakens much earlier than that of non-smokers.
- The colour of the face becomes pale and yellow due to less inhalation of oxygen. The teeth and lips too become yellowish and stained.
- The immune system weakens, due to which smokers are prone to diseases such as excessive bouts of cold and cough, asthma, and other respiratory problems.
- Ulcers in the digestive system are aggravated by smoking and medicine too fails to cure them. Smokers are highly prone to premature wrinkled skin.

- Smoking weakens bones and women who smoke reach menopause at an early age.
- The chances of cancer are increased ten times in smokers as compared to non-smokers.
- The chances of cancer double when smoking is accompanied by the consumption of alcohol.
- Women who smoke have 60% danger of having a miscarriage. Apart from the development of congenital diseases, asthma and respiratory diseases are also found in the children of such mothers. The height of these children is also less at the time of birth.
- Passive (indirect) smokers also are prone to the dangers and risks that smokers are exposed to. Passive smoking is as harmful as active smoking.

The following can be considered to quit smoking:

- Will power plays a big role in quitting any addiction. Inform your family and friends that you have decided to give up smoking. Use them as your support system to quit.
- Consume juices and go on fasts.
- Practice *yogasana* and *pranayama*. Place a small piece of *harad* in your mouth. Whenever you feel the desire to smoke, chew on cardamom (*elaichi*) or clove.
- Once you succeed in quitting smoking, do not begin again. As time passes the desire to smoke will decrease and eventually you will not even think of smoking again.

Alcohol (liquor or hard drink)

Do not consume alcohol for amusement. When it is regularly consumed as a source of amusement, it becomes an addiction and ruins the life of the consumer. An addict finds and makes all sorts of excuses to procure alcohol. The desire for alcohol overpowers all reasoning and the person does not hesitate to lie or make false promises to obtain it.

Disadvantages of alcohol consumption

- Physical and mental disorders occur as a result of excessive alcohol intake; at times illegal means are adopted to procure it and this may induce a person to be involved in criminal activity.
- Alcohol is the base of mental sickness. It may be the cause of neurological, liver, and gastric disorders.
- The danger for heart attack increases with excessive alcohol intake. Liquor addiction disturbs family peace and may result, at times, in domestic violence.
- Liquor addiction is worse than cancer. With cancer only the patient suffers but with alcohol addiction the entire family suffers.
- Ethyl alcohol, the alcohol that is used in liquor, has a tendency to dissolve in human blood. This is the reason why all organs of the body get affected by alcohol consumption. Prolonged use of liquor causes liver cirrhosis, which takes a long time to cure. Ethyl alcohol is also responsible for digestive problems.

To get rid of the habit of alcohol consumption

- Giving up drinking requires inner strength and a change in attitude. A determined person can surely free himself from the addiction of liquor. Drinking the juice of orange and lemon and eating fruits such as apples and bananas helps reduce the toxins accumulated in the body due to the consumption of alcohol.
- Dates are very useful in curing alcohol addiction. Soak 3–4 dates in half a glass of water. When they soften, lightly rub them in the soaked water. Drinking this water helps

reduce alcohol addiction. This water should be taken twice a day for one month.

- Add a pinch of *ajwain* (aniseed/anise) in half a glass of water and stir it well. Sieve this and drink this water daily for one month; this too helps in reducing alcohol addiction.
- Stop smoking immediately. Smoking increases the desire of alcohol consumption.
- Cleanse the digestive canal with *kunjal*, enema, or *shankh-prakshalana*.
- Practice yoga regularly. It enhances self-confidence and reduces the dependence on intoxicants. *Gyan mudra* and *trataka* (*dhyan*) in particular are very helpful.

Drugs

Any substance that alters the mental status of a person and induces sleep or brings about an intoxicated state is called a narcotic or drug.

All intoxicants at first are taken occasionally. With the passage of time the urge to take more of it increases and this habit then gradually becomes an addiction. To become dependent on a fixed habit either physically or mentally is called addiction. A person who becomes addicted to some habit, especially to the use of a narcotic drug is called an addict.

Addiction to drugs can cause the following:

- The habit of intoxicating one's self may result in criminal activity because drugs are expensive.
- An addict loses all control over his life and future. He becomes dependent on others who make choices for him.
- The efficiency of a person decreases when a person is under the effect of drugs.

- As the procurement of narcotics is expensive, addicts often end up losing their personal belongings such as their house or vehicle as well as their status in society. They are usually held responsible for criminal activity and may land up in jail. Consumption of several kinds of drugs leads to various infections in the body.
- Under the influence of drugs, addicts may end up practicing unsafe sex and suffer from unwanted pregnancy as well as increase the possibilities of venereal infectious diseases and HIV/AIDS.

For rehabilitation do the following

- Occasional fasting is beneficial.
- Eat fruits, salads, and sprouts in large quantities every day. Include spinach, cabbage, white goose poot (*bathua*), coriander, mint leaves, radish leaves, turnip leaves, or any other edible leaves in your meals daily. Take care that the leaves are washed properly. Consume 100–200 grams of any of these leaves daily; this helps in reducing drug addiction.
- Applying mud pack on the stomach helps the body get rid of toxins. Also helpful are regular enemas, *kunjal, neti, kapal bhati, shankh prakshalan*, etc.
- Practice breathing exercises such as pranayama and tratak
- For professional guidance contact any of the drug rehabilitation centres in your city/town.

The following help in the identification of a drug addict

1. Low attendance in school, college, office, or factory.
2. Stays awake till late night without any reason.
3. Makes new friends and leaves old ones.
4. Increases expenditure or demands more money to spend.

5. Gets annoyed without any reason and display abnormal behaviour.
6. Marked tiredness, laziness, and restlessness with trembling in the body, excessive sweating, and an expressionless face.
7. Swelling below eyes; sticky or bloodshot eyes.
8. No interest in social activities and constant feeling of weakness.
9. Disturbed sleep and frequent changes in the time and manner of sleeping.
10. Reduction in digestion power, weight, and patience.
11. Frequent habit of borrowing or stealing money (missing of things from house).
12. Unnecessarily tells lies.
13. Traces of burnt marks on the clothes or on the body.
14. Abdominal spasms and constipation.
15. Displays eccentric behaviour and has misleading thoughts.
16. Presence of long cardboards, paper strips, unfamiliar powder, etc. in the house.
17. Presence of injections or syringes in the house.
18. New or multiple injection marks on the body.
19. Loves to stay alone and spends long hours in the washroom.
20. Tends to forget the words spoken and ends up speaking nonsense or idle talk.

Parents of addicts should do the following

1. Assure that the child's health is fine and he is eating properly, is having sufficient sleep, and is exercising regularly.

2. Parents and teachers should interact with each other and help the child as well as each other for curing the intoxication.
3. Getting health checkups done at fixed intervals is a good habit.
4. Encourage your child to be involved in physical activity, to exercise, and to participate in outdoor games and sports.
5. Spend quality time with the child and fix a period of family time (maybe during dinner) when the family can interact and work out each others problems.
6. Do not be liberal with pocket money; instead give love in abundance.
7. Do not merely cater to your child's physical needs; try and fulfil his mental needs as well and thus promote security in him.
8. Involve children in domestic activities.
9. Children like discipline because it means that parents are paying attention to them.
10. Discuss the problems being faced by children in school in a calm and mature manner.
11. Do not put unnecessary pressure or burden on children that cannot be fulfilled.
12. Always be determined and behave in a decent manner in the presence of children.

Date Rape and What Is "Date Rape"

These are drugs that used in a sexual assault. When they are used, the victim may:

- Be physically helpless
- Be unable to refuse sex
- May not remember what happened.

These drugs often have no colour, smell or taste, and are easily added to flavoured drinks without the victim's knowledge. All traces of these drugs exit the body within 72 hours of ingestion and cannot be found in any routine toxicology screen or blood test.

In date rape the following drugs are used

- GHB (gamma hydroxybutyric acid): it has a few forms – liquid with no odour or colour, white powder, and pills. Street names include "Liquid G", "G", "Georgia Home Boy", "Easy Lay", and "Grievous Bodily Harm".
- Rohypnol (flunitrazepam) is a pill that dissolves in liquids. Street names are "roofies" or "roaches".
- Ketamine (ketamine hydrochloride) is a white powder. Street names include "K", "Vitamin K", or "Special K".

How to protect yourself from date rape drugs

- Do not accept drinks from anyone.
- Unseal bottles, cans, and containers of your drinks yourself.
- Keep your drink with you at all times, even when you go to the washroom.
- Never share drinks.
- Avoid drinking from punch bowls or other large, common, and open containers. They may have drugs in them.
- Be aware of your surroundings.
- Be aware of the street names of drugs.
- Trust your instincts. If you feel ill, get help immediately.
- Do not drink anything that tastes or smells strange.
- Have a nondrinking friend accompany you to make sure nothing untoward happens.

Jealousy

Jealousy or envy is of two kinds.

One is positive envy that motivates us to become like other successful people by adopting their good values.

The other is negative envy in which we get troubled by others' success and while hating them act negatively against them.

When a person is filled with negative envy, he is unable to see the well being of the other person and cannot tolerate his success. He unnecessarily criticises successful people, makes false allegations, and always tries to devalue the work done by them.

Usually a person who is jealous describes the work of successful people a game of destiny to make their success seem less valued.

This is sad but true. We are more unhappy by others' happiness than we are happy by our own happiness. This is increasingly visible in todays so called "modern" society. We suffer because our neighbours, relatives, acquaintances are doing well and are happy. Their happiness is so disturbing to us that we waste our valuable time and energy in constantly trying to pull them down, instead of using our energy trying to do something worthwhile that may make us successful. Therefore, being jealous in fact puts a stop to our personal growth and we feel defeated. So, not only is it important to prevent yourself from being jealous of others, but to also try and protect yourself from the jealous eyes of others.

It is better to concentrate on making ourselves stronger, than to waste our time and energy in taking revenge.

Stay away from people who do not respect your ambitions, and avoid discussing your success with such people.

Do not make the mistake of boasting your wealth or lifestyle to people who are weaker than you.

Save yourself from the jealousy of people by discussing your problems with them.

At times it becomes difficult to save yourself from being the victim of someone else's jealousy. In such a situation always keep yourself busy in your work.

Dissatisfaction is indeed the mother of jealousy. A person who either does satisfactory work or is satisfied with his position in his office will surely will be saved from the fire of envy.

To check yourself from being jealous of others, try and focus on the individual's positive and strong values, pick them up and try to develop them as your own.

If you always compare yourself with others, then you will surely be the victim of ego or jealousy.

Criticism

As often seen, a jealous person will also be a critic. He constantly finds fault with almost everything and is never happy to see other people being successful and happy in their lives.

People who constantly criticise have damaged personalities, also called "personality disorder". Such people are never happy and they begrudge others' their happiness too. Criticism is done with the intention to insult or defame someone.

Psychiatrists and yoga experts believe that people who are idle and who possess no creativity are the ones who waste their time in criticising others. They have no work to occupy themselves and hence no plans for their future. Through criticism they vent their negative feelings and thoughts, wasting valuable time and their lives in idle chatter. Backbiting and criticising become their life and they get trapped in this vicious wheel. Criticism has the potential to degrade even the positive and good people. It is believed that a critic is not trustworthy enough to be anyone's friend or confidante. People stop believing in him, because they are not sure when he may end up criticising his own friends. He loses out on true friends and suffers from the ill effects of fault finding. Try not to focus too much on the negative characteristics in a person. Every person possesses some good qualities. Always concentrate on the positive qualities of the other person. Attempt to adopt these positive qualities and avoid being influenced by the negative characteristics. If you are aware that you possess some of these negative points, try and give them up. People with a negative mind are the ones who always find faults in others. Remember, none of us are perfect; we all have faults. So, it is unfair to criticise others when we ourselves are at fault.

When you do come across someone who criticises others, try and avoid them if possible, but if you do have to listen then refrain from commenting. People who criticise others in front of you will surely criticise you in front of others. Every word of criticism uttered becomes a mountain of an obstacle in the way of your success. Words of criticism spread like fire in every direction and at some time or the other will for sure reach the person who has been criticised. The actual words usually become deformed before they reach the person, who is then sure to turn against you. If you must criticise, then criticize the action and not the person. Always focus on the positive qualities of others and analyse the faults that you possess. This way not only will you be able to benefit from the positive qualities of others, but will also work on your own positive qualities. Refrain from wasting your priceless time and energy in criticizing others. Instead put it in your efforts towards constructive work and in living a respectful life full of success and excellence.

Never get furious when you hear others criticise you; understand that a critic is your friend. By criticising us he in turn does us good, by helping us see our shortcomings. And, if we focus on our faults and work on them positively we will surely be winners!

Effect of Society (Company)

A person is recognized by the company he keeps. An individual adopts the ideologies of the persons he mingles with or from the material he reads. So the identity of a person depends on the kind of people he is associated with.

It is better to stay alone rather than in the company of negative and immoral people.

Bad company has the ability to leave an impact on the wisest of persons; just like when one goes into a coal mine all clean but emerges with black smears on the clean clothes. One can never escape the scars received by the company of corrupt and evil individuals. But, the reverse is also true.

Good company has the power to alter even the most corrupt and evil individuals and also encourages them to reform themselves.

Keeping good company can be helpful throughout one's life — during times of difficulties and distress, when faced by adversities, or in situations that require the taking of harsh and severe decisions.

It is better to stay in a jungle with a good companion rather than to stay in a palace with a bad companion. With a good companion not only is there a change in the conscious mind, but there is positive change in the unconscious mind too. With the positive encouragement that one gets, the attitude changes and things in life get a new meaning with countless possibilities.

Just as flowers spread their fragrance, humans too emit magnetic waves of ideologies and feelings. Pure and clear conscience people have a calm and spiritual feeling around them. By being in the presence of such beings, our thoughts become virtuous and free from past disagreeable circumstances; such is their influence on us.

Falsehood and Truth

We make a lot of mistakes in our daily lives, and then we lie to hide them. At first it may seem that lying helps, but if we keep lying to cover our mistakes we will never be able to correct them. Sometimes people lie to save from being punished or people in business lie to gain profits. Lies do not remain hidden for long; they get exposed very quickly. To be safe avoid resorting to lies no matter how difficult the situation. Sticking to the truth in the long-run always helps. A person who lies can never be trusted. To blame others unreasonably or to criticise them is also considered a lie.

The main difference between a truth and a lie is that the truth can be spoken repeatedly, but not lies. This is because when people lie they usually forget what lies they had spoken earlier and so end up mixing their facts. Hence, to catch a liar ask him the same question again and again. And if there are different answers then it will be easily proved that he is telling lies.

People who regularly lie are usually very clever; they tend to talk less when they tell a lie. They know that by talking too much they may speak about something that may expose their lie. But, sometimes people begin to talk more to hide their lie. They start giving clarifications even before being asked. The change in their talk and behaviour is enough to suggest that they are lying.

Some of the signs that a person is lying are: people while lying may abnormally perspire; they display abnormal behaviour; there are changes of expression on their faces when they lie; at times the way of talking changes. Some other signs are: rubbing the hands while talking; scratching the floor with the toes; chewing on nails; crackling of fingers;

running the fingers through one's hair; twitching of neck; or clearing of throat. All these signs suggest that the person is not behaving normal and is trying to misguide others by lying.

We agree that lying is a bad habit and should not be encouraged, but on the other hand we should also try and find out what is making a person lie. A person who is telling lies should be listened to and heard carefully to understand the reason for his resorting to lies. Sometimes recognising the reason behind a lie makes it more helpful to figure out what the real situation is than if the truth were spoken.

When you know of a person who is close to you and is lying, take him into confidence and try to understand the reason behind his telling the lie. Usually spouses lie to each other or children lie to their parents or teachers. This may happen because of emotional distress or the fear of insecurity. In such situations it is extremely important to help them find an amicable solution that strengthens their bond and does not encourage them to resort to lies. This is all the more important if children are the ones lying. Parents should talk to them freely and try to understand the reason they are lying. Once the reason is clear, parents should try and solve the problem for which the lie was told. Sometimes they may need to take the help of the child's teacher too.

Truth is that which is real, agreeable, non-hypocritical and does not harm anyone.

Enmity

Ego, anger, hatred, a selfish attitude, and other such vices are the mother of enmity. People who are jealous by the success of others or those who are self-centred and egoistical give rise to enmity.

Tolerance teaches a person to be thoughtful and prevents him from unnecessary suffering and distress; this in the long run leads him to success and destroys the feeling of enmity and hatred within him.

Avoid arguing with your friends, companions, and family. Do not tell them "you are wrong". Try not to irritate them or accuse them for no reason. It is actions such as these that lead to people making enemies.

The best and the safest option is to just go ahead and compromise with a difficult person to escape from unnecessary confrontations and eventually feelings of enmity.

The best way to make your enemy favourable is to love him.

People who hate you will not win till the moment you don't hate them.

When we make enemies then we prepare ourselves for ailments such as hypertension, insomnia, frustration, etc. These conditions not only make us unhealthy and ill, but also affect our happiness and peace.

One of the characteristics of antagonistic people is their revengeful nature. The best protection against such people is your conduct; have a positive attitude and display good behaviour at all times.

Our competitor is our best helper. Our struggle with the problems keeps us aware of our objectives. Our competitor compels us to remain attached to our mission, objectives, and goals from every angle. It is only because of our competitor that we are not only able to see the surface but also become eligible to touch the depths.

Loneliness

Loneliness or solitude not only makes us unhappy but it also causes harm to both the body and the mind. A study found that loneliness is as bad for health as obesity and smoking. It not only leads to the development of a sad mentality, but it also negatively affects many regions of the brain. Loneliness causes blood pressure and stress to increase. A lonely person at times suffers from reduced will power and self-restraint. This may lead to depression which then begins to affect his entire life. People have been known to eat more when depressed or be disinterested in interacting or even leading a healthy an active life. Such a condition leads to life-threatening illnesses and people spend unhappy lives.

Loneliness may be avoided in the following ways

1. Stay in touch with your family. If possible, visit friends and relatives. If not, at least stay in touch by calling each other once in a while or by meeting and interacting online.
2. Make reading a habit. It keeps the brain busy and active, and one is also able to collect information about new and interesting things.
3. Exercise and go for morning walks regularly. They strengthen the immune system and as a result protect you against a lot of diseases.
4. If possible join a group that engages in activities that interest you — travelling, reading, music, etc. This not only reduces your loneliness but also helps you be in touch with people from various walks of life.

5. Engage in activities that benefit the society at large. People who do social service for at least two hours a week have less episodes of depression and also remain healthy, both physically and mentally.

Boredom

Boredom means when a person finds the day-to-day activities monotonous and tiresome. A bored person feels irritated, lacks interest, and at times is indifferent and angry. Humans are the only living beings who suffer from the feeling of boredom.

Normally boredom is of two types: short termed and long termed. The short-timed boredom is one which lasts only for a short duration, such as waiting for someone to arrive or waiting in a long queue. Long-termed boredom is more like a chronic disease that lasts for a fairly long duration. This is a serious condition that can have a negative and unfavourable effect on life and make it meaningless. Life becomes dull and the constant boredom proves to be destructive. It destroys the very existence of an individual.

Reasons of Boredom Aimlessness

With no goal or aim to look forward to, an individual loses all charm in life and tends to go astray. One begins to think that life is not progressing because of the lack of a purpose or objective.

Lack of personal interest

Individuals feel bored when they are involved in activities that do not interest them. Personal interests usually vary, and tasks become tiresome and difficult when not done with interest.

Work system

Every person tries to find simplicity, easiness, and perceptibility in his work system, and feels bored in the absence of any of these.

Monotony

Any activity that continues permanently without any change or newness creates a condition of boredom.

Lack of punctuality

When work is not completed on time, it increases the waiting period and this waiting period gives rise to boredom.

To avoid boredom

The following three questions can be raised in a situation of boredom:

1. How will these situations help me go ahead in life?
2. In these situations can I help someone else too?
3. In such circumstances what would a wiser person have done?

Try to find out the answers to these and avoid boredom.

A person gets tired not by the abundance of work done by him but by considering the work a burden and doing it irregularly.

Fear

There is nothing dangerous and bad in life than fear. We are never defeated by anything else in life but by our own fear.

Types of Fear

Fear is of different types. Every person suffers from different kinds of fears. Some people fear situations and incidents. Some may fear other people and some have fears that are unfounded; having fears of disturbances that have not even occurred.

Reasons For Fear

A person has no fears at birth. Over the years, as he grows and depending on the parenting and upbringing he receives, he develops various fears. These fears get engrained in the young mind and as the child grows his fears increase. And, if the child is brought up in a house or community that has false beliefs and faith in superstitions, the child develops fears that are baseless and useless, and which trouble him for life. Children whose childhood has passed under difficult circumstances sometimes develop fears that haunt them for years. Even if their situation improves when they grow up, they fear a repetition of childhood events.

Very young children sometimes develop fears after reading or listening to horror stories and events, or after seeing scary movies. When a child is assaulted or scolded by an individual on multiple occasions, the child develops fears that cause mental harm and may interfere in the child's healthy upbringing. Sometimes parents in the process of trying to correct their children's negative habits, intimidate them into following a positive behaviour and end up building scary ideas and unfounded fears in their children's minds.

Usually people develop fear in their minds by being convinced that they will fail in their work or job, not realising that it is the fear that causes the failure.

To succeed one has to throw the fear or cause of fear completely out of their minds, otherwise it is almost impossible to succeed in anything.

Results of Fear

People with a weak mind are the ones who are subjected to fear; they are exploited by hypocrites who use and frighten them in the name of religion and superstition. Fearful people remain self-centered, suffer from inferiority complex with no proper development in personality, mostly remain at the back in the race of life, miss out on good opportunities, and become an object of fun and ridicule.

Ignorance and lack of specific knowledge sometimes lead to heightening of fear. For instance in the absence of proper sex education at the school or college level, many youngsters step into the adult world with widespread misconceptions because of which they are unable to build or endure their sexual relationships, both mentally and physically, with their partners and due to lack of facts many end up consultation quacks to understand their problems.

How To Become Fearless

One of the most dependable and easy ways to destroy fear from its root is to repeatedly carry out the work or act that frightens you. Gradually with each repeat the fear will continue to decrease and then finally disappear.

A busy person does not have the time to fear or fill his head with useless thoughts. It is the idle mind that conjures up situations and actions that fill fear in the mind of the person. To fight fear and make it go away completely, try and develop self-confidence, consciously stay away from superstitions and false beliefs, do not allow challenges or changes in life frighten you, and remain positive as much as possible. Also, try and develop friendships with fearless people. Once a person begins to believe that there is nothing to fear and be tense in this world, his life becomes easy and practical.

For doing or not doing a particular work, fear is a strong and powerful motivator. To use it properly one needs to avoid doing any wrong work or action and not be afraid to do any rightful work or action.

Hesitation

To be hesitant doubtful or uncertain about things shows lack of self-confidence and thus makes your personality incomplete. A shy or hesitant person may possess all the other positive qualities but being doubtful sets him back as compared to others who are outgoing. A shy person is not able to explain himself clearly and completely, and so most of the times is ignored by people around him, which makes him lonely, hopeless, and worrisome. Despite being talented and capable he is not able to come forward and display his skills. But it is not difficult to overcome shyness.

Once you decide to work towards it fix a target for yourself that you will at least speak a line or two with every person you meet. Even if it is just to ask the time or the address or the bus route number. You may also discuss things like the weather or the good things happening in your city; but, every day keep a target of talking a few lines to every person you meet. First the need is to meet people; next is to interact and hold a short talk with them. If meeting people on a daily basis is not possible then join some club where you will get the opportunity to meet lots of people to discuss issues of your interest. Also try to attend social functions when invited; never turn down invitations; and if possible hold small gatherings yourself. If you get an opportunity to address a group of people, take full advantage of the situation. Gradually your hesitation will decrease and you will be freed from the habit of shyness.

Hurry and Rashness

As the saying goes, haste is waste. Usually people hurry and the result becomes adverse; from getting work done early it gets delayed, and the work is disorganised and faulty. A person in a hurry is always full of rashness. He hurries while eating; rushes to work, to go somewhere, or to talk and the result is that the work gets damaged instead of getting right.

Hurriedness and rashness are resorted to when people desire success in a relatively short time than is possible. They do not want to put in long hours of hard work and labour to achieve success, and in the want for instant success they adopt improper and unfair means.

To be successful at something it requires patience and perseverance. But, people who desire success instantly are always in a hurry, and when they are not able to get success the way they had planned they become frustrated. They keep shifting from one work to the other in the hope of achieving success, not realising that until they see the work through with patience, success will not be possible. What they need to understand is that every work undertaken takes a certain amount of time before it can be successful.

Letting go of it before it reaches that point will never result in success. All it will result in is a waste of their money, time, and labour. These somewhat impatient people have a lot of passion towards their work but lack steadiness. They want everything all at once, and when they do not get it they are disappointed. As a short cut they turn to Godmen and holy men for their divine blessings and boons of divinity and incantation. Success cannot be achieved in any work without putting in time and labour. There is no route to success that has no obstacles or difficulties. To remove these barriers from the path to success, a lot of effort and patience is needed. Today or tomorrow, tomorrow or the day after tomorrow, a hard working and determined person will surely taste success; and, even if after all the hard work and pains he is unsuccessful due to some reason, he will not be a loser. The effort and time that he has devoted to the work will surely have resulted in enhancing his skills and abilities. His personality gets honed and all this in the long run results in success. Hence, it is said that work once undertaken should be done with full concentration and continuity, and there should not be any delay or haste.

The biggest obstacle in the path of success is impatience. Working with patience and courage helps you in moving in the appropriate direction to success.

Unnecessary Interference

Nature has made everything unique and incomparable. Things of the same group differ. Even two stones are not same. Therefore, finding similarities between two individuals is impossible. Every person has unique and rare characteristics – different hobbies, different nature, different likes and dislikes and so on. These differences do not become a reason of conflict outside the family but they do create conflicts within the family. Apparently all quarrels and conflicts in a family are due to the difference in behaviour and nature of two individuals.

When people do not create an atmosphere of adjusting with one another according to each person's nature or behaviour, the tendency of interference arises; and, if the interference is unusual then a conflict arises. Excessive and unnecessary interference has been seen to be the main reason for conflicts in families. Some such interventions include, spouses interfering in each other's matter without being asked too; children interfering into their parent's matters; siblings interfering and causing unnecessary impediments for each other. Sometimes parents interfere into their adult children's lives and create demanding situations that are difficult to handle.

Not all interference can be called bad or negative. If an individual is involved in some unethical or illegal activity, it is very important to interfere and discourage him from going

Such a kind of person is definitely a victim of ignorance who answers without being asked.

ahead with the plans, or otherwise the family may have to pay for the consequences. A family that respects each other's opinions, beliefs, likes and dislikes, values, and innocent habits creates an atmosphere of friendship and happiness in the family.

Mobile

Cell phones or mobiles have become a necessity in today's hectic and fast-paced life, without which we cannot imagine spending a single day of our lives. Earlier mobile phones were considered status symbols but now anyone and everyone can be seen talking on one.

Scientific studies and researches have shown that the radiation waves being emitted from mobile phones are harmful and affect our health. General survey and examinations have shown that the prolonged and continued use of mobile phones can cause cancer, blood pressure, ear tumours, weakness of memory, skin diseases, and in some cases impotency in males. The electromagnetic waves that are emitted from mobile phones not only have a bad effect on the user but also on the people near the user. Children in particular suffer immensely from the ill effects of the electromagnetic waves.

Apart from the ill effects cell phones have on our body, a lot of time and energy is wasted in unnecessary and idle talk. Also, unscrupulous and fraudulent people use mobile phones to spread rumours that at times result in drastic and uncontrollable situations. The nation as a whole suffers. But, this does not mean mobile phones are evil and should not be used. If used in a sensible and constructive manner, cell phones can make our daily lives very easy and smooth.

While using them it is beneficial to follow some precautions. Try and keep the phone at a safe distance from the ear and while talking if possible use the left ear. It is safer to avoid the right ear, because the memory part of the brain is just above the right ear.

Do not hold the mobile phone between the head and the shoulder; instead hold it with your hand. This does not cause unnecessary strain to the neck.

To prevent unnecessary complications in your life and lifestyle, use the mobile phone only when it is extremely necessary to do so.

Television

Watching television is an integral part of our lives be it the elderly or children, male or female, rich or poor, all alike. In spite of being an extremely convenient and inexpensive source of entertainment, watching television in excess is harmful and invites ailments. Given here are some of the harmful effects of watching television.

Anyone who watches television sitting too close to it for prolonged periods can develop conditions of irritability, insomnia, stress, epilepsy, obesity, and depression.

The rays that are emitted from televisions are damaging and cause unnecessary harm. They block the functioning system of the brain of little children, because their brains are still in the stage of development. According to a report school children who watch television for two or more hours, face the danger of suffering from increased cholesterol in their body. Also, too much of television watching increases the chances of vision loss, dizziness, and quick mental tiredness.

The power of thinking becomes dull, there is loss of memory and creative power, and the person gets exhausted faster than usual. Avoid watching television while having meals, because it is harmful to health.

Television should not be watched before going to sleep. It affects our subconscious mind and the mind becomes disturbed which has destructive and hazardous effects on the body.

Languor of Spirit

Languor of spirit is a feeling of the mind that develops by excess of sins done either knowingly or unknowingly, or by mistake or due to negligence. Every person repents for his sins and bad activities that he does during his lifetime, which is also necessary but within limits. When a person makes a resolution not to repeat his mistakes in future, then there is a strong effort to reform his mistakes by remaining away from sins. During such a time, the act of repentance helps a person to be released from his sins; but if it exceeds its limits, the person suffers from languor of spirit.

Such a person gives undue importance to the smallest of mistakes made by him, continuously remains in shame and sorrow, and gets distressed mentally as if he were the culprit. He constantly curses himself remembering the mistakes committed by him due to ignorance and innocence, and always remains sad.

In a state of languor of spirit, the person constantly thinks of himself as a sinner and an immoral being. Due to this inferiority complex, he wastes his talents and creativity, which leads to no substantial improvement. Such people are not able to present themselves properly, and always remain irritated and dissatisfied. They remain immersed in disturbing thoughts and suffer from various physical and mental diseases. No doubt, these people remain in languor of spirit throughout their life. Significant possibilities of their life that could have been achieved come to an abrupt end. Their ambitions, hopes, desires, and abundance wither away before time. There are many intelligent and talented young people who destroy their lives by falling victim to languor of spirit.

To avoid being negatively affected by failures and mistakes committed by you, try and forget all the bad done by you. Do not let the languor of spirit increase inside you otherwise it will become a mental disorder from which you will find it difficult to emerge. Do not allow the feelings of wrong doing of the past adversely affect you. Avoid shame, fear, and hesitation; forget past sins and develop self-confidence, and courage and make your life successful.

Uncontrolled Ambitions

Ambition is a campaign full of courage and activity to make excellence, greatness, ideals, a reality in which a healthy and balanced mind, awakened consciousness, and judicious intelligence works and opens the doors of surprising successes in this world. A life without ambitions becomes worthless and the doors of world development close. Today the progressive development that the world sees is because of the result of the ambitions of many people put together. It is only because of them that the doors of great scientific researches and wonders in the world have opened.

But when we are unable to realise our ambitions and fulfil them, our lives become uncomfortable and there is a feeling of pain and dissatisfaction.

Unfulfilled ambitions usually play a major role in corrupting our outlook towards our ultimate goal. From following the simple and proper way to achieve our goal, they mislead us into following the easy but wrong way. Because of which we ignore what we should be doing and instead begin to concentrate on improper and unfair means to reach our goal and fulfil our ambitions. When our aspirations are realised by unsuitable means, we tend to become arrogant and haughty in our approach towards life. We begin increasing our prosperity merely to satisfy our ego. Real and true prosperity comes from good habits, sincere efforts, and persistent labour. But a person dominated by ego is not capable of walking on this simple path; he adopts the path of immortality and dishonesty.

He resorts to pride and greed; both are close companions of each other. If pride is there, greed cannot be far behind.

Being ambitious is not a bad thing, but we should use our discrimination and judgement while considering our aspirations and ambitiousness. Are they useful and realistic? Are we under some kind of deception? Are our ambitions leading us on the right path of life or making us stray away from the path of righteousness? Is there any kind of temptation or selfish thought behind our ambitions? Try and be careful while considering an exceptionally good offer. Decide your answer by focussing on some of these questions – is it too good to be true? Why am I being made this offer? Do I really deserve this or is there some ulterior motive behind this? Is someone with a selfish mind behind this?

Be cautious if someone is trying to attract you towards a highly profitable deal. Do not fail to judge the danger within such a deal. Remember that if something is being provided to you easily then it can be demanded with a high value in the future. If possible, try to avoid unearned profits.

Ambitions are the motivations of human lives. In the absence of ambitions the speed of life decreases. It is wise to examine our ambitions on the criteria of truth and reality, and evaluate on the basis of merits and demerits.

Dissatisfaction

Dissatisfaction from anything causes a damaging defeat. Usually dissatisfaction arises due to jealousy. When a person sees someone richer, stronger, or of dignity more than him, he starts thinking that the other person is happier, accomplished, and is more honourable in the society than him. Along with jealousy, dissatisfaction is also born which leads to demerits one after another.

Just as every person has both positive and negative qualities, joy and sorrow also co-exist. The only difference is that someone has one kind of joy and sorrow while someone else has another kind. All these are ever changing. Every person is better than the other in some activity or the other.

Some people are unnecessarily dissatisfied from the atmosphere of their own families. They feel other families enjoy more comforts and peace. Such people who see only deficiencies and defects around them cannot experience any peace or joy in their life.

A person who remains satisfied with whatever he possesses and does not run after things that he does not have or wishes to have is not only intelligent but also sensible. External situations cannot affect him because he is content with his situation. To lead a happy life one should be satisfied with whatever one has been provided with. He should understand the importance of it and enjoy it.

The secret to success and happiness is to learn to live by observing people who live their lives within limited means, and to set ones goals by being inspired by people who have lived a progressive and prosperous life.

Try to compare yourself with only yourself. Make improvements in yourself and in your work every day, so that one day you are able to walk on the path to success. Then, there will be no reason for dissatisfaction.

Character Formation

An individual's character forms the base of his stable and successful life. Success achieved without character does not last very long. Our character is formed by the work we do, our behaviour, the kinds of thoughts we have, and our mentality or attitude — all qualities that we have nurtured in our entire life.

History proves that prosperity, fame, and dignity follow a person whose character is strong and firm. Such people are never alone at unfortunate times in their lives. People go out of the way to help them. But a characterless person does not make long-lasting friends; even their so-called closest friends become strangers in time of need.

A characterless person cannot be successful in the long-run. He may for a short time gain some prosperity or fame, but in the long run he will always remain empty. His spirit will always be low. He will forever be longing for pleasure, fearlessness, self-dependence, and satisfaction. His conscience will always trouble him and his mind will be restless.

A characterless person will be frightened of the society, his family members, and at times of himself too.

To build a strong character, control the negative thoughts that arise in the mind. Do not run away from difficulties, face them. Only then will possessing a good character become a reality.

Listening to religious discourses or moral teachings, are useful and help in building a positive character.

Just like every brick is important while building a house, in the same way every thought that crosses one's mind is important in building a strong character.

Patience

Patience is the truth of life. A real winner is one who patiently bears and accepts difficulties in life.

Patience is necessary for maintaining joy and peace in our family as well as around us at all times. We must develop it to an extent where we have the capability to listen and bear criticism peacefully even if it is presented cruelly to us. If someone is angry with you and uses derogatory language against you, try not to get excited. Face the person with positivity without any thought of enmity. Try to focus on the positive side of the person; every person has some good in him.

No person remains the same all his life.

The test of the limit of your patience is by observing yourself and analysing your tolerance level. Till the time you feel that you are tolerating a lot, it means you are still trying to find patience; you have not become completely patient yet.

When a stone wants to become something, he hands himself over to the person who has a chisel and a hammer.

Forgiveness

If we hold a feeling of anger, complaint, enmity, or hostility against someone, then we are bound to bear the pain of this damaging mentality. But once we forgive the other person for his faults and flaws, our mind is set free and we no longer remain distressed or anguished. If we follow the path of peace, love, friendship, cooperation, and affection in our lives instead of anger, hate, and indifferences, we will be able to live a worry-free life that has no unnecessary concerns or anxieties. A simple meaning of forgiveness is to keep yourself fit and disease-free. Study and scientific research have proved that the person who is forgiving remains healthy in the long run and is also free from diseases and illnesses. He even recovers faster if he is ill and ailing. The person who learns to forgive also learns to control many afflictions.

Forgiving and asking for forgiveness are both equally important; they destroy the ego of both sides. Asking for forgiveness means getting freedom from false ego; people with a big ego never ask for forgiveness. Such people are neither capable of forgiving anyone nor can they ask for forgiveness from anyone. The person who forgives and the person who asks for forgiveness, both are considered generous. Forgiveness ends enmity and expands friendship.

Forgiveness is possible in every condition, whether one asks to be forgiven or not. You can free your ego by forgiving a person even if the other person is not asking for forgiveness. Why continue to carry the burden of others' mistakes in your mind? Making a person realise his mistakes in the right way, even if he is not asking for forgiveness, gives a chance to the other person to work and improve on his own behaviour.

Morality

Your behaviour is the test of your morality.

Anyone who is kind is a favourite with everyone, because kindness is a quality that gives birth to other positive qualities as well as leads to prosperity.

It is the law of nature that anything that is productive and yielding has the tendency to bow and bend to nature. Similarly, gentle and kind individuals who live a life of virtue tend to be more adjustable in life; they are considerate and courteous in difficult situations and also adaptable.

Wherever there is authenticity there is belief and faith.

The search for faithful and devoted people is everywhere. They can be trusted with major responsibilities and the biggest contributions can be made by them too. It is important that you maintain the faith of others and try to fulfil all the promises made by you to others. If you want to be a good speaker then you should be a good listener. If you want to be a good writer then you should be a good reader. If you want to be a good teacher then you should be a good student. If you want to be a good king then you should be a good citizen. If you want to be a good master then you should be a good server. If you move ahead in life with these thoughts in mind, you will be able to become a good and positive person.

The worst thing in life is that tears come in someone's eyes because of you.

The best thing in life is that tears come in someone's eyes for you.

The Art of Donation

In simple words, love, charity, and kindness are all various kinds of donations. The best donation is to give to an underprivileged person, such as feeding the hungry, providing clothing to the unclothed, and if possible providing shelter to the homeless. These activities bear fruit if done without any expectations.

An actual donation is one in which the donor donates but does not know himself that he is donating. He must not have any grand feeling of donating, nor any ego or expectation for the fruits of donation.

The donation that has expectation, publicity, and ego associated with it cannot be an actual donation; it is considered a mere business transaction.

The greatest service is to help a needy become self-dependent.

An ideal donor is one who by his presence and contacts makes people so capable and self-dependent that in times to come they will never need to take monetary donation from anyone.

Another kind of donation that you can give to a person is that of education. Feed the hungry today and he will be hungry again tomorrow. But, instead educate and train him so that he becomes self-reliant and responsible enough to live his life independently. We cannot make a person accomplished and self-dependent by providing alms. Equip him to live his life respectfully by earning his own livelihood. Donations made towards the welfare of the society are obviously the best gift one can give. Some of the activities that one contribute towards are the building of rest houses, construction of schools and colleges, digging of new wells and reconstruction of the old ones, etc.

Today there are many lazy and worthless people who beg for donations and then later drink and gamble the money away. These irresponsible and wasted individuals have no aim in life and merely increase the crime and corruption in the country. Avoid donating to these parasites of our society.

Some donations do not require us to contribute monetarily. They are as important and useful as the monetary donations that we make – the donation of a kind word, of labour (for public works), of happiness, of our precious time, of forgiveness, of fearlessness, etc.

A donation through which someone's life can be saved or a new life can be given is called the supreme donation. Some such donations are:

Blood Donation

There is no substitute of human blood; it can be replaced only by blood. You can donate blood if:

- your age is more than 18 years and less than 60 years (for both men and women)
- your weight is at least 45 kg
- your pulse and blood pressure are appropriate
- your haemoglobin (Hb) is a minimum of 12.5 gm/dl
- there is a gap of 3 months between two blood donations.

The Indian Red Cross Blood Bank is one of the many organisations that provides the requisite infrastructure for blood donation.

The Indian Red Cross Blood Bank also sets up various camps for receiving donated blood. (Red Cross Road, New Delhi–110001; Phone No.: 23711551, 23716441; Timings: 8 a.m. to 8 p.m., all days of the week)

Apart from this organisation, you can go to any hospital to donate blood.

Eye Donation

Eye donation is also considered supreme donation because it not only provides a person with eyesight, but also changes his life completely.

During eye donation, the corneas are taken out from a dead person's eyes and provided to two blind persons. Cornea is the glass-like covering over the pupil of the eye. The cornea is removed instead of the complete eye so that the dead person's face does not get damaged. By eye donation, the eye sight of two blind people is restored.

Any person can donate eyes. Even those persons who have cataract or have had some surgery of the eyes or are using spectacles can donate their eyes.

No living person can donate eyes. It is only possible once a person is dead.

When a family member expires then it is the wish of the family members and at times the deceased may express such desire when alive to donate his eyes. The family can then inform a nearby eye bank and can donate the eyes, although the deceased, when alive, would not have signed the eye donation form. Eye donation procedure takes about 10–15 minutes and can be done either in the hospital, residence, or any other place where the body has been kept.

Eyes can be donated to only those who suffer from corneal blindness and not to those who suffer from retinal complaints or from problems in the nerve and interior structure of the eye. A person should be at least 18 years old to sign up for eye donation. Eyes can be donated above the age of one without distinction of religion, caste, or status.

If you are willing to donate your eyes, let your family members, friends, lawyer, family doctor, or any other person close to you know about your wishes, so that no obstacles come in the way of your auspicious act of eye donation. If you do not inform your family, relatives, or friends about your wish to donate your eyes, they may not be able inform the eye bank on time and then it may become too late. Let your willingness be known so that your eyes are able to light up two lives.

Inspire your relatives and friends too to sign up for eye donation. When someone you know expires, inform his family and relatives about eye donation and encourage them to donate the eyes of the deceased. If they agree, immediately contact the eye bank and complete the necessary formalities.

Eyes can be donated until 6 hours after death. Hence, it is essential to contact the nearest eye bank immediately. Eye banks function 24x7. To make sure that the eyes are suitable for donation keep the following in mind: do not switch on the fan (you can switch on the air conditioner); shut the eye lids and keep a wet towel on them or you can even keep a cube of ice wrapped in a towel on the eye lids.

You and your family can pledge to donate your eyes during your lifetime. Why wait; take the decision now.

Organ Donation: Organ donation is the process of donating those organs that can be transplanted in the body of another person after the death of the donor.

Today science has advanced so much that important organs such as bones, skin, few soft tissues, kidneys, liver, heart, lungs, pancreas, middle ear, etc., can be transplanted easily.

After blood, the most transplantable tissue is bone. Hip bone, thigh bone, elbow, knee, and many other damaged bones can be replaced with the bone received from organ donation.

By agreeing to donate our organs we continue to be of use to society even after our death. There are no ill effects on the body after organ donation, nor are there any complications during the funeral.

Organ donation can take place only after one is declared "brain dead".

The meaning of brain death is that the whole body is alive but the brain becomes inactive of all its functions.

This stage is accepted as death throughout the world and the Supreme Court of India too recognises it. Brain death is declared by a special team of doctors. Organs should be transplanted within 24 hours of brain death.

A brain dead person can be kept in this position for a long time with the help of some life-saving instruments, glucose, and oxygen. Many of his organs can be used for transplantation.

For self-organ donation one must fill a form. There should be two witnesses and one of them should be a close relative.

Role of Organ Retrieval Banking Organisation

Organ Retrieval Banking Organisation (ORBO) makes organ transplantation a reality. A nodal centre for the nation, ORBO has been set up at the All India Institute of Medical Sciences (AIIMS), New Delhi, with a purpose of encouraging organ donations, and for the fair and equitable distribution and optimum utilisation of human organs. The organisation maintains a waiting list of terminally ill patients requiring transplants, donor registration, matching of recipients with donor, and co-ordination from procurement of the organs to the transplantation, dissemination of information to concerned hospitals, organisations and individuals, to creating awareness, promotion of organ donation and transplantation activities.

Your vital organs will be transplanted into an individual who needs them most urgently. Organs are matched to the recipient on the basis of medical suitability and the urgency of transplantation according to the waiting list and geographical location.

Note: Help line for organ donation 1060 (open 24 hours).

All India Institute of Medical Sciences

Ansari Nagar, New Delhi-110029
Ph.: 91-11-26593444 - 25688360 Fax : 91-11-26588402 E-mail id: orboindia@yahoo.com; Website: www.orbo.org.in

ORGAN DONOR FORM

Date .... Regn. No. ....

I, ...son / daughter / wife of ....in the hope that I may help others, hereby make this anatomical gift, if medically acceptable, to take effect upon my brain death. I hereby wish to donate the following organs: Heart, Lungs, Kidneys, Liver, Corneas &

....

My blood group is ....

Special wishes, if any ....

Signed by the Donor in the presence of two witnesses:

....

Signature of Donor with date Date of Birth of Donor

Address of Donor ....

....

Telephone No. . ...

E-mail : ....

Witness .... Witness ....

Name .... Name ....

Add .... Add ....

Tel.: .... Tel.: ....

Correct Decisions

Taking decisions is an art and not being able to take decisions is more or less a dangerous disease. Innumerable hurdles and difficulties come in the way of taking the right decision at the right time. At times decisions are taken without all the information being present and so we end up sometimes taking decisions in uncertainty. What would be its result would be known only in the future. Such situations sometimes baffle and confuse us and at such a time we are not sure of ourselves or our decisions. Most times we suffer because we lose out on opportunities only because we either said a quick "no" or replied with a late "yes". While taking a decision, discrimination, experience, perception, imagination, and value, are all important.

The positive and negative effects of all options must be thoroughly analysed. What will be the advantages and disadvantages of every option? In what way will they contribute to achieving our goal? These are some of the questions one should ask and then accordingly choose the best option.

Once we have reached a decision, we should immediately start working on it. Do not wait to review or re-think it. Excessive thinking creates confusion.

Try and avoid the wrong decisions that you have taken in the past and learn from others' mistakes. Use those experiences to help you take correct decisions in the future.

Precautions

1. **Do not take decisions in haste**: Some people have a habit of taking the most important decisions very quickly without consideration and without caring

for results. Problems arise when their decisions turn to be wrong in the future and they have no choice left but to repent.

2. **Do not take decisions emotionally or sentimentally**: Many times, because of the circumstances we are in, we become emotional. In such a situation, our mind loses the power of thinking, consideration, and understanding and then whatever decision we take turns out to be wrong. Try not to take any important decisions when too excited or emotional Instead try to take important decisions with patience and by not being swayed by emotions or sentiments.
3. **Do not let your ego come in between while taking decisions**: Sometimes with the interference of ego a small problem that could easily have been solved becomes a big problem. We make it an issue of defeat and victory. Because of the presence of ego, we sometimes take such decisions for which we repent later. Hence, do not let ego interfere with your decisions.
4. **Do not take decisions by asking others**: It is usually seen that people avoid taking decisions themselves and instead ask others as to what they should do. They do so because they do not want to bear the responsibility of the results. The first and most important thing to consider here is that no one knows your problems better than you. Second, you may get mislead because people may give you wrong advice due to their own interests or may misguide you out of jealousy. Be self-dependent and decide for yourself how you want things to be in your life.
5. **Do not be obstinate while taking decisions**: After taking a decision, if you manage to gather more information that affects your decision, do not hesitate to change your decision and take a new one. This

should not make you feel ashamed or lead you to think what people will say about you. Actions corrected and taken on time always yield better results than delayed and inflexible actions.

6. **Do not take decisions in anger**: Decisions taken in anger have been found to be incorrect most of the time.

Habits

You cannot change others. You cannot change your parents, spouse, brothers, sisters, or your boss. All you can do is change yourself.

When you change yourself, you change your surroundings along with it.

First, we make our habits and then habits make us. Whenever we do something regularly for up to 21 days, it becomes our habit. Develop habits that strengthen you and build your personality. Some of such habits are:

1. Be punctual.
2. Keep your word.
3. Complete the work that has been started by you.
4. Do your work with interest.
5. Be happy.
6. Be excited.
7. Drink two to four glasses of water early in the morning.
8. Sprinkle your eyes with the mouth filled with water.
9. Clean your palates (upper part of mouth) every day.
10. Press your jaws while defecating.

After the accomplishment of one habit proceed to the next.

Slowly, as you proceed from one habit to the next you will realise that each habit gradually becomes a part of your life and that you do not require any extra effort to maintain it. By applying this method, in one year you will have developed many habits that will slowly become a part of your life as well as contribute to your overall success in life.

For example, you should write at least five pages a day if you want to become a writer.

Just as good habits can be developed to become a part of our life, so can bad habits be given up. All that is needed is a strong will to follow through.

Resolution

Taking a firm decision to do something beneficial is known as a resolution. If possible make resolution on special days of your life: on New Year's Day, on your birthday, when celebrating your wedding anniversary, on festivals, when on a pilgrimage, etc.

Make a resolution to give up inferior habits: Resolve that you will let go of ill habits that harm you the most, such as consuming hard drinks, smoking, gambling, needless spending, anger, jealousy, etc.

Make a resolution to adopt good qualities: Resolve to adopt good qualities that are most important to you, such as time management, positive thinking, saving, etc.

Make a resolution to complete unfinished work: Resolve that you will stop procrastinating tasks and will complete all pending work. Lingering wastes time and uses up a lot of the positive energy. Ignoring unfinished tasks leads to a restless mind that is constantly burdened by the thought of having to complete the task. The moment an effort is made to complete the pending work, the pent-up energy in the body gets released and a feeling of achievement is gained.

The world belongs to the person who has patience and certainty.

Social Service

Social service or welfare work or serving the needy, is a noble and selfless way of serving your fellowmen. Every person finds success when he is supported by the public; without public support he is helpless. Man is a social animal. We cannot have mastery and control on all aspects of our life. To be able to concentrate on one aspect of life, we require help of each other so that the other aspects of our lives are taken care of. We can never be totally and completely self-dependent for all our worldly needs.

We can consider ourselves similar to a drop in the ocean of humanity. Can a single brick build a house? Similarly we all co-exist and try to become a single ocean of life.

We take from someone and we give back to someone. To help and serve others is a part of our lives. Even materialistic success cannot be achieved without the assistance of a large number of people in our lives. This also means that our life becomes comfortable when we are helped by other people. The life of the richest person also depends on somebody else's help. True social service is one that aids in the success, improvement, and advancement of the people of our society.

There are many works in society that cannot be completed by government machinery alone. Helpful people and social organisations need to come forward. Some such activities are:

Teaching the illiterate

It should be the aim of every literate Indian citizen that no child remains illiterate in our country. Each and every person in our country deserves at least minimum education, and it is people like us who can do this. The fulfilment of this mission will surely elevate the society to a new literate level.

A large number of grownup men and women too remain illiterate throughout their lives. Educated and literate people in our society can take it upon them to teach such people and equip them with basic reading and writing skills. This can be done by opening schools for grownups. Such schools can be operational during the nights and mornings in all towns and villages.

Discouraging costly wedding affairs

The trend of having big and costly weddings has lead to the people becoming financially and ethically irresponsible.

The pressure to hold costly weddings forces people to earn larger amounts of money either by adopting wrong means or by compromising their basic necessities such as food, clothes, medicine, education, etc. People end up in huge debts when they borrow money from the banks or through the money lenders. Because not everyone can afford a big and expensive wedding ceremony thousands of girls either remain unmarried or are married off to old men; some women even commit suicide. If all this money were to be saved by conducting small and simple ceremonies, the financial status of our nation would be much better in the international scene. Increase of income is beneficial only when misspending is controlled otherwise financial problems will remain the same.

Discouraging the habit of intoxication

A lot of money in our society is wasted by people to fulfil their desire of being intoxicated. If this money could be saved, problems of health, education, homelessness, etc., could be met and the evils of sickness, family disputes, and crimes that are all linked to financial crises could be eliminated.

Avoiding discrimination on the basis of caste

There is a huge need today for us to join as one within the bond of similarity and unity that has otherwise been scattered in different castes for many years now.

Providing good libraries

A library is an important means to increase and upgrade knowledge for a literate person. Not all of us can afford to buy all the books. Libraries solve this problem. There is a need for good libraries that promote good reading habits and encourage people to enhance their knowledge. Mobile libraries too can fill this gap.

Eradicating beggary

Beggary has made millions of people idle. A person who is unskilled prefers begging to working. Begging is easy money, no matter what the amount. To end this curse on society, beggars must be discouraged from begging and be forced to work. If a person is disabled or physically challenged, he has to be provided work that suits him rather than be allowed to beg. Begging is a shame and the sight of beggars a disgrace to the country.

Eliminating superstitious beliefs

If we do not help in eliminating baseless superstitions and false beliefs from our society, we will forever be dogged by them.

Note: The chapter mentions only some services that one can do to selflessly serve the society. But, there are many other things that can be done for individual and public development.

Social Relations

Try to develop a liking for people and after some time you will be able to generate a genuine liking for them.

If you feel that the other person does not remember your name, reintroduce yourself. While introducing yourself smile and shake hands with enthusiasm with the other person.

Try and meet new people in ceremonies and get-togethers.

If there are some people who you particularly wish to meet, then tell a person close to them to introduce you to them.

Remember the names of the people you know and have met before and use their names while conversing with them.

Take genuine interest in other people. Ask "happy" questions and discuss things that make people feel joyful. Encourage them to talk on subjects and topics they feel happy talking about.

The way to touch a person's heart is to talk about those things that are most important to him.

Touching someone's heart means making the other person realise in a refined way that you accept his importance with a true heart.

By arguing and debating with a person you may win over him but you will fail to win him over or win his heart.

When you meet new people who you want to develop relations with, try and maintain contact with them by calling and writing to them. Never give up on a chance to congratulate others on their success and always condole and sympathize in moments of sadness and grief.

Self-Motivation

To attain our maximum capability we must motivate ourselves. Self-motivation cannot be achieved without applying pressure on ourselves. Nothing will happen if someone else applies pressure on us.

Try and understand your values and principles in life; think that you are the most important person on the planet.

If you are able to recognise your inner powers, the world too will be able to identify and acknowledge them.

Being born poor or average is not a curse, but dying with average talents is pitiful. It is a shame if during your lifetime you are not able to raise the level of your capabilities and put your talents to use.

No one must die an average person. Every person should strive to reveal his inner genius and must try and use his talents to rise to the highest rungs of success.

We cannot change time but we must know when it is time to change ourselves.

Every great person was once a helpless child and every skyscraper was once a blueprint. Where you are today is not as important as what you want to be in the times to come.

Try to spread your own wings to fly, because you will be unable to fly depending on others' wings.

Always remind yourself that you were born to do some great work.

The biggest challenge in life is the completion of the task that people thought you would not be able to do.

Be an ideal for others in any field of activity, be it social service, a job in some organisation, or your own business that you are involved in. Let your actions speak for themselves, not your words.

Ponder on the following and if possible adopt some of them:

- Don't be weak; no one wants to be the friend of a weak person
- Become the deserving one, not the demanding one
- Believe in things rather than being suspicious
- Be hard-working and industrious; it is easy to be lazy and indifferent
- Save money and value its worth
- Complete the work that you have started no matter how tough; avoid lazy and sluggish people who are not serious and who do not follow through with their responsibilities. In other words have the courage to do something different.

To self-motivate it is important to do a self-analysis. Estimate your talents and defects honestly. Such an exercise of self-analysis would strengthen your aims and encourage you to move forward on your path to success.

Avoid comparing yourself with others. Do not get distracted while fixing your goal. A perfect person is one who contests with himself.

Recognise yourself.
Recognise your powers and believe that you will win.

Self-Control

Self-control, or restraint, is the biggest security and power one can possess in life. One who wins over others is strong but the one who wins over himself is powerful. *Kshatriya* King, Vishwamitra became *Brahmarishi* by the power of self-control.

A person with no self-control cannot pass even the smallest exam of character. Self-control is the base of character.

Organ Control

The five sense organs are – eyes: to see; ears: to hear; nose: to smell; tongue: to taste; skin: to touch and feel.

The five organs of actions are – hands, legs, vocal cords, excretory organs, respiratory organs.

Misuse of any of these organs displays lack of self-control.

Financial Control

Use money in a proper and, if possible, serviceable way instead of wasting it.

Control of Time

Make sure time is put to the maximum use through proper time management.

Control of Thoughts

When negative thoughts occur try to shift focus from them, and make an effort to keep your thoughts positive and creative.

Nothing is impossible for the person who has the following controls – control of speech, control over mind, control over anger, control over hunger, control on desires, control over taste.

Enjoyment is an art. The real joy of life is achieved only when we include self-control and patience in our journey of life. Enjoy the things or moments or qualities that you possess and try to derive genuine happiness and pleasure from them.

What is important to remember is that true self-control is tested only in an adverse situation. Let's take the example of an honest person. A person who has never been dishonest cannot be called an honest person just because he has not been dishonest ever. He would be called honest only when presented with a situation to be honest he refuses to stray and adopts a path of honesty. This is a truly honest man.

A person who is poor or unable to earn his livelihood becomes a saint. A vigourless person becomes a *Brahmachari*. A person suffering from incurable diseases becomes a devotee of God and starts devotion. An old lady becomes faithful to her husband. The actual importance of adopting *brahmacharya* is to become inept even when being capable; freeing oneself from worldly attachment even when being wealthy; becoming a devotee of God even when being healthy; and being faithful to your husband even when being young and beautiful.

– Chanakya

Self-Confidence

Anything can be obtained with self-confidence.

Self-confidence has so much power; if one decides to engage in some work that seems impossible at first, with self-confidence the work can be achieved in life sometime or the other.

If one has the confidence that even in the presence of difficulties he will taken on work, then it is this self-confidence of his that helps him go ahead in any direction and face difficulties, but in the end be victorious. His self-confidence should be so fixed and firm that he should not get distracted from his goal of victory.

All men or women, who have achieved high positions and statuses, have one common quality — self-confidence. Self-confidence and the ability to take a firm decision are the most important factors for success.

We all go through painful situations and have to fight against difficulties, problems, and inconveniences in life. Our self-confidence gives us a release from these problems. All one needs is to take sensible decisions and then stand firm on them no matter what. People who lack self-confidence waste all their talents and qualifications, because they do not have the confidence to use their qualities to move ahead in life. Self-confidence not only makes life better but also strengthens our personality. Some people lack self-confidence from childhood, while some people change with circumstances and their sour experiences in life.

There is a great difference between self-confidence and pride. The base of pride is materialistic desires and mental disorders. Self-confidence gives rise to endeavour.

Increase your self-confidence

Prepare a list of your hobbies and talents. Write with full honesty those things that you like, your qualities that influence people and make them happy. Write these down and read them regularly. This will result in an increase in your self-confidence.

Increase your positive qualities

Every person should attempt to increase their positive qualities even if it is patience, forgiveness, listening patiently to others, or endurance. Widen your thought process; don't keep your thoughts restricted and don't get captivated in rituals and superstitions.

Read inspiring books and autobiographies and try to adopt them in your life.

Read the character sketches of great people from whom you derive inspiration to live a better life. Reading and learning inspiring quotes can get you out of the most difficult situations.

Get rid of your fear

There can be no self-confidence where there is fear. Take a pen and paper and write all your fears on it, such as your fear of public speaking, fear of meeting and interacting with people, fear of mingling with new people, fear of conversing in English, fear of driving a vehicle, etc. Discuss these fears with yourself and try to work on them and win them over one at a time. Do not run away from your fears; face them. Once you are able to win over one of your fears, you will find your fears decreasing and your self-confidence increasing.

Learn the art of speaking well

Our talks and our way of talking are important; they not only influence and attract people, they also increase our self-confidence. If you fear talking in front of others, try standing in front of a mirror and talking to yourself. This will reduce your hesitation and increase your self-confidence. Learn to say "Yes" or "No" at the right time so that you do not repent later.

Keep all the information and material related to the topic you are going to talk on ready and well prepared. Read a lot and increase your general knowledge. Reflect on language, grammar and style of talking, and listen to others. Become a patient and good listener. Then, try to speak to yourself and practice it to perfect it.

Be an expert in any one activity

No one is absolutely perfect. To be self–confident it is not necessary that you be the best in everything you do. Choose any one activity and display your ability and talent in that particular activity. Make it the ladder of your identity and self-confidence. Even a single activity done with confidence and expertise is enough to give rise to self-confidence.

Learn the art of dressing well and appropriately

Wearing your best and dressing appropriately for an occasion increases self-confidence. The best dress is one that looks on you and is also comfortable to wear.

Take the front row

Many people prefer to sit in the last bench in schools, offices, and meetings. The reason of this is that they do not want to make themselves prominent and so try to avoid attention. Lack of self-confidence is the biggest cause for this. To avoid this, sit in the front row so that others may notice you. This will rid you of your baseless fear and lead to an increase in your self-confidence. Many people do not speak or share their ideas in meetings, seminars, and discussions. They feel that if they make a mistake people will take them to be a fool. Do not fear of making mistakes. Learn to gain confidence from your mistakes and add them to your experiences.

Recognise your talents

Every person is talented; each one of us has one talent or the other. If we search within we will surely hit upon some hidden talent. This talent if worked on can help us make a mark in society as well as in the people's hearts. So try to identify your talents and increase your self-confidence.

Avoid procrastination and learn to complete your work

Work that is complete makes us happy and increases our self-confidence whereas incomplete work decreases our self-confidence and makes us dejected and depressed. If we continue to procrastinate and fail to complete our work then we being to believe that we can never complete our tasks. The "I can't do anything" feeling is very harmful and it also decreases our self-confidence. Never consider your work to be a burden or "headache." This will reduce your stress and you will be able to do your work happily and satisfactorily. Your self-confidence too will increase and you will be able to complete the work in a proper way and within the appropriate time.

We should have 100% confidence in ourselves. If you can learn to create new ideas every second, you will be able to see new enthusiasm being created within yourself. The result of self-confidence is authentic. The world believes in a person who believes in himself.

Self-Analysis

Self-analysis is a very useful tool. Humans should always think where is the flow of period? Try and consider the following questions: Who are my friends? Who are my enemies? One should always maintain a personal record of his income and expenses.

It is also useful to estimate your abilities and weaknesses and accordingly decide the work that is favourable and can be done successfully.

Do something different

Every activity after a certain point of time gets monotonous. Cut down this monotony in your work by try to do something new and something different from time to time.

When we get bored it decreases our capacity to work and perform and also hampers our capabilities. Hence, by trying out different things you generate excitement and rejuvenation and also give birth to new ideas.

The challenge of the new ideas also instigate you to do something new and at times such activities reveal your hidden talents and abilities. You begin to feel your power, thoughts, and abilities widening and strengthening.

Ask favourable questions to yourself

Only if you ask suitable questions to yourself will you get favourable answers. Your focus strengthens by doing this and you view things in a positive light.
Some of these questions are:

1. Which things make you happy?
2. Which is the thing that makes you feel proud?

3. Who are the people to whom you are obliged?
4. Which work do you do best?
5. What good habits do you possess?
6. Which habits do you want to improve on?
7. Which person has helped you the most?

In the beginning people do not even believe that something new can be done. As time passes they begin to think that it is not possible to do such a thing. But, later when they watch that work being done by others and being made possible, then they begin to think why it was not done earlier.

Enhance Soft Skills

For a successful professional apart from having academic qualifications, his quality of behaviour is also as important. Such qualities are known as "soft skills".

The characteristics of your personality that qualify as soft skills are: displaying confidence and enthusiasm while shaking hands with colleagues or visitors; smiling genuinely and sweetly; good time management skills; positive and optimistic thinking; and so on. Candidates who exhibit their soft skills along with the knowledge in their field of expertise stand a better chance at interviews and at times also excel in them. Every skill and talent is considered important in today's job market. Some of these are: belief, reliability, determination, craze or passion, faithfulness, imaginary power, self-motivation, and the wish to learn new things and adapt to new situations.

Most employers believe that if you want to build your career in a planned way then you should have the following qualities – art of working with good coordination with others; ability to lead a team; quick power presentation skills for issues and things related to the workplace; good communication, both in written and verbal forms; the skill to present your points concisely in a meeting or boardroom by speaking in a clear and fluent manner; the ability to recognise the problems at work and being able to find their solutions; to prepare favourable modules for the team to achieve the decided goals; adopting behavioural skills as and how the situation demands; being computer and techno savvy.

Only the wish to achieve perfection instead of "good enough" can take a person to the best desired position.

Professional/Professionalism

A professional is a person who is highly skilled and trained in his sphere of work. Having the qualities of a professional is called professionalism. We should all strive to be professionals.

Requisites For Being A Professional Are

1. **Dedication:** Being completely dedicated to your work and profession leads to acquiring popularity and honour in your organisation. This is not only beneficial to you but also helps in setting an example of commitment to the rest of the team.
2. **Upgrade and update knowledge:** Update your professional knowledge from time to time. Be aware of the new things happening in your line of work and whenever required take a course or a program that helps you refresh your knowledge.
3. **Participate in seminars, workshops, etc.:** It is not possible for a person to learn everything on his own. One learns a lot by participating in seminars, conventions, meetings, etc. This also gives you an opportunity to interact with people who are also involved in your sphere of work.
4. **Educate others:** Just as it is important to educate yourself about your work, it is also necessary to inform and educate others about the benefits and scope in your profession.
5. **Continuous improvement:** Aim for including continuous betterment in your work. Both you and your team need to be put through this exercise – researching new techniques for sales, learning and forming new ideologies, finding new customers, etc.

The work of a professional is to

1. Focus on the needs and benefits of his customers or clients.
2. Give the same response to both small and large customers.
3. Take regular care of the changing needs of his customers.
4. Be always ready to help, especially in times of crises.
5. Develop a habit of working in a regular and organised manner within his team.
6. Develop a method of being specific with the work and clients.
7. Be always punctual and encourage his team to do the same.
8. Know the art of balanced living.

Qualities of a professional

1. Self-disciplined
2. Determined
3. Healthy
4. Good character
5. Good communication skills
6. Time management
7. Knowledge
8. Self-confidence
9. Positive mentality
10. Integrity
11. Good habits
12. Dedication

The best reputation that one can earn is being praised by his competitors.

Workaholic

If you are being troubled by sitting idle for a short period of time then certainly you are a workaholic. Such people never feel relaxed; they think it is a waste of time to sleep or entertain one's self. Mostly their discussions are related to their work, and if someone tries to discuss other things, they steer the conversation back to work. Workaholism is an addiction.

Just as excessive consumption of alcohol is an addiction, so is the habit to do too much work. The ill effects of being a workaholic are clearly evident on the mental and physical health of a person as well as in his social life. Such type of people acquire problems such as stress, frustration, depression, loneliness, a weak memory, blood pressure, diabetes, unbearable pain, and a weak immune system. Apart from these, such people are unable to adjust in their social lives. They cannot properly handle relationships and take no part in social activities. They also find it difficult to spend quality time with their families.

The desire to have everything in life in a short time, the yearning for praise and promotions, and other such aspirations create passions in people to do more work that later becomes excessive and begins to interfere with their everyday lives. However, to lead a good life one must maintain a balance between professional and personal life. Not only that, one must also give importance to adequate rest. Until and unless one is relaxed and cool, they cannot work properly. This means that work and rest are both deeply related to each other, and by maintaining a balance between the two the best performance can be achieved.

Rest

Just as exercise is necessary for maintaining good health, in the same way rest too is important for a good health.

Proper rest helps restore energy spent in doing hard work. There is no solution other than rest for tiredness.

Both physical and mental rest are necessary. Hence, only with the sufficient rest of both will there be a state of complete rest.

Sleep is the best source of rest.

For short-term rest do *shavasana*.

Usually, people take physical rest but remain far away from mental rest. Mental rest can be done by turning off mental work, closing the eyes, and being calm and tension-free. Try this in the office: close your eyes for a few minutes; cup your hands and keep them on eyes with your elbows placed on the desk. This is the best way of getting some mental rest.

Keeping a wet-sheet pack of icy cold water on the eyes helps remove tiredness of the eyes.

Meditation too gives rest to the mind.

Keeping silent for short spells is also a good means of resting yourself.

If possible, keep taking rest, weather mental or physical, every 3 hours. By doing this, energy for doing work increases.

Physical and mental ailments result if proper rest is not taken Complete rest is the best medicine.

Note: Beginning of lack of interest in work is a signal of the requirement of complete rest.

Pleasure

To experience pleasure is easy but defining it is a tough job. Knowing, understanding, feeling the ultimate mystery of pleasure is different for each one of us. We all have different expressions towards it. If a little child is asked what gives him the most pleasure, he would simply say that he likes the most to be in his mother's lap. If the same is asked to a youth, the answer would be "to complete his education with good marks". If a married person is asked he would most probably say that he would like "to live a good life with his family", and if the same is asked to an old person the answer would be that he would like "to return to his youth days". Some people get pleasure in giving and some get pleasure in taking.

Pleasure is that situation in which your mind starts "dancing", and our lips start to hum automatically. Our heart gets a flood wave of happiness.

In the modern world, life has become a race that makes us behave like machines. In such a situation even when great successes are achieved they do not result in real happiness or satisfaction. People continue to feel lonely and lost. Though they are comfortable in their lives, there is a general feeling of dissatisfaction.

The true reason for such a state of affairs is that though these "successful" people live comfortable lives, their lives lack any genuine pleasures. In the absence of pleasure all successes become valueless, because one is knowingly forgoing pleasure. Try to think of one thing that gives you the most pleasure. If things such as, dancing, listening to music, or painting give you pleasure and positive energy, adopt them as a hobby. Get involved in things that interest you. Sometimes there are small things that give pleasure, such as collecting photos of childhood. Keeping them carefully preserved and seeing them from time to time brings back sweet old memories.

Any activity that is done if regarded as a burden cannot be truly enjoyed. If you do any work considering it to be necessary then you will enjoy the work.

Entertainment

To be healthy and happy in life entertainment is necessary.

An act that satisfies you and gladdens your heart is called healthy entertainment.

Entertainment and happiness make us stress free. They help us forget our problems in life and we strive to be happy and healthy.

Entertainment also frees us from acts of jealousy, envy, fear, anger, dissatisfaction, and worry.

The possibility of mental illness increases in the absence of entertainment.

Hence, we should all take time out for entertainment

Entertainment can be done in any one of the following methods

1. Laughing is the best and easy source of entertainment. Laugh and keep stress away.
2. Every day clap, be happy, be healthy, and scare away diseases.
3. Play your favourite music. Experience the enjoyment of listening to music.
4. Refresh you mind by singing in the shower; any song that you like and enjoy or one that which comes automatically to you.
5. Maintain a journal. Write thoughts that come to your mind and read good writings. This stabilises your mind and helps you focus on your goals.
6. Enjoy the environment — walk in green areas, sit by the river, watch the waves of the sea or stare at the stars at night.

7. Spend quality time with your family. Become a child with your children.
8. Keep meeting those you enjoy being with and those who like you. Love is not only the best expression in the world but it is also a beautiful experience.
9. Keep pets if possible. Activities of animals are often astonishing and entertaining as well.
10. Walking, doing *yogasana* and exercising, playing sports, etc., are important and healthy activities for the body and mind. They keep you busy and entertained.
11. Being involved in activities, such as cycling, horse riding, painting, swimming, gardening, and photography are some of the pursuits that one can follow for entertainment and happiness.

Sure, life is tough, but it is nothing to be taken so seriously. Strive to life a happy life between all the worries and pains. Try to meet people, go for walks, try to entertain yourself by adopting new hobbies, try to find the child inside you and become like him; live your life in good spirits and whenever possible avoid tensions and stressors. Do not tie yourself to formalities, rules, laws, superstitions, etc. Keep yourself free. Enjoy life. Keep yourself assured that by living a free and happy life you are doing good not only for yourself, but also for the people around you. Your life too has an aim or a goal. When you realise that your life is your own, you will be a satisfied person.

Dance, it is an important means of entertainment. Dance also has an importance in keeping us fit and healthy. It leads to a development in intelligence and physical beauty. While dancing there is physical and mental coordination between all the organs of the body because of which the day-to-day tensions are released. Dance is done not only for happiness but it is also a kind of exercise.

Responsibility

A duty is assigned and a responsibility is assumed. Reliable and worthy individuals focus on their responsibilities, whereas lazy and worthless people persist on their rights.

Assuming responsibilities and accomplishing them successfully is what results in progress and achievements in life. Responsibilities tend to enhance our capabilities and knowledge to successfully move ahead in life.

A responsible person is self-dependent, while an irresponsible person is forever dependent on others. Irresponsible people never take responsibility for their mistakes. They constantly look for excuses to blame others. To become a responsible individual strive to improve on your failures rather than blaming others for them.

It is our duty to help our children become self-dependent and responsible by allowing them to handle some of the everyday burdens.

We must not blame others for our mistakes or failure. We can only improve them when we take the responsibility for our mistakes and failures.

Our responsibilities are

1. Towards ourselves
2. Towards our family
3. Towards our colleagues
4. Towards our clients
5. Towards our organisation
6. Towards our society

7. Towards our nation
8. Towards our environment

These should be considered our duties that need to be accomplished well and we should do everything possible to fulfil them.

Effective Leadership

You can be the leader of your house, an industry, a social organisation, or of the country, but to be a successful leader you need to be an effective leader too.

Effective leadership is not about only delivering lectures but it is also about delivering positive results.

Best leadership comes from taking responsibilities. A responsible person become a good leader.

A leader has to take correct and tough decisions at all levels which is an important skill. A leader who is good with this automatically excels.

Behind every successful business there is a tough decision that was taken by someone at some point of time.

To become a good leader:

1. Appreciate others for their co-operation
2. Give importance to others' thoughts and experience
3. Be a good and patient listener
4. Implement positive thoughts
5. Develop a positive and creative thinking
6. Have farsightedness
7. Inculcate a habit of encouraging others
8. Become an expert at communication.

Always remember: A culture begins from top to bottom, not bottom to top.

If you want to learn something, teach it to others. While teaching, you will learn new things yourself. Thus, the person who teaches others learns the most.

Time Management

God has given only 24 hours to every person. It depends on the capability of a person how he utilises these 24 hours skilfully. For this, recognition of the right time and organising appropriate work at the appropriate time is necessary. This is called time management. One who is skilled at time management would also manage his life well.

Lost wealth can be regained, forgotten education can again be re-learned, lost health can be brought back through treatment, but lost time cannot be regained by any method. One can only repent.

Just as money is used to buy material things, in the same way time is used to buy education, wisdom, wealth, fame, health, peace, and freedom. We have been sent on this Earth with an abundant wealth of time and have been given the freedom to buy anything that is of interest in this universe in exchange of time. People who value time spend it like the valuable pearls of life.

Your future depends on how you spend the time allotted to you. . When we say that we do not have time to do a particular thing, it means that we do not know how to use time and manage it well.

The balance and the proper use of time

- Give time to think – this is the source of strength
- Give time to play – this is the secret of youth
- Give time to studies – this is the fountain of knowledge
- Give time to work – this is the key to success
- Give time to friendship – this is the path to joy

- Give time to family — this is the storage of happiness
- Give time to sufficient sleep — this is necessary for health
- Give time to personality development — this is the art of living

Divide different times of the day for different works

- Divide your tasks according to priority
- Pre-plan your daily activities
- If you prefer to think at night, then plan at night for the next day. If you prefer to think in the morning then plan your day just after rising from bed. While making a plan for all necessary works of the day never forget to keep some spare time for some sudden work and rest.
- Complete an important work before it becomes the most important work
- People who do their work earlier or at the right time never fall short of time
- The meaning of panic is equal to saving a few minutes by wasting hours
- The best time to do anything is now
- If you wait for a particular time or occasion to start a task, the work will never get started
- Never follow your mood while starting any work. This means that we should not do our work according to the mood we are in but instead work according to our aims and plans
- Never procrastinate. By deferring work or not doing it on time, time is wasted and the work gets delayed further
- Even a small amount of work done at the right time proves to be beneficial, and a great work not done at the right time goes to waste

- If we make it a habit to wake up early in the morning, we will be surprised that how this small habit affects our daily thoughts, works, and time management of the entire day.

Create time

- Do some small task in the time between two big tasks. For instance, travelling time can be used for planning. Such planning saves time
- Always keep a substitute option for waiting time – reading books related to goal or health
- Always talk to the point. The right conversation saves time
- Delegate all the works to paid workers except the work that should be done by you
- Use necessary infrastructures, such as the phone, email, computer, etc., to cut down on time wastage and use time as desired
- Some of the works that waste time in our day-to-day life are sitting in front of the television for long hours, having useless and extended conversations on the phone, reading the newspaper from beginning to end, gossiping, etc.
- Select news, magazines, books, television programmes that interest you and avoid the rest. Use the phone to discuss only important topics
- When you move out of the house, ponder for a few minutes and try and decide what other works could also be done while you are out. Instead of wasting time in idle chatter, cursing the world, and gossiping, try to exchange good ideas among yourselves. When we take interest in our work then the work is completed easily but the work in which we have less interest, takes a long time to be completed. Hence it is said, that a person is

lucky if he loves his job because he can do more work in less time and can also do the work more efficiently, because of which he becomes successful professionally

Be organised

- From time to time weed out the useless things in your home and office
- Clutter and waste papers increase stress; discard them
- Always keep your things at a proper place, so that it is easier to retrieve them, instead of wasting time looking for them
- Adopt a proper filing system to keep like things together. Try to regularly organise every task in your home and your office; disorganised works takes more time than organised work
- Always take an appointment before meeting someone. If you have not taken an appointment then it is possible that you will be waiting unnecessarily and wasting your valuable time. It is also possible that you may not get to meet the person and your time of travel would also be wasted
- Whatever work you are doing, do it with complete concentration
- Carry a paper and pen with you at all times, because as soon as you get an idea you can jot it down
- Always keep some time aside from your daily schedule to learn the work that you always wanted to do
- Keep in mind that if your daily routine is organised then your life will also be organised
- When you feel that there is no work pending then you should involve yourself in chores, such as cleaning, arrangement of clothes, house repairs, gardening, write-

ups, topic discussions, or reading some useful literature, etc. You can also use your time to take care of broken articles, receive health care, and increase your knowledge. You cannot evaluate time by money only. There are so many charitable activities to get involved in and we should make it our duty to perform them. The result of devoting time in virtuous works is always pleasant.

The basic cause of physical or mental ailments of most people is their mismanagement of time.

Art of Communication

The art of exchanging messages between two or more people is called communication. This includes things, such as exchange of thoughts, perception of body and mind, expression of emotions, etc.

Means of communication are

1. Verbal
2. Written
3. Body language
4. Mass communication

The use of body language in communication tells us how the other person is feeling while listening to you

Feeling:

55 percent depends on body language

38 percent depends on your tone or level of voice

7 percent depends on your words and sentences

For effective communication the following are necessary – mental efforts, toleration, sympathy and talent. No work of a person can be completed without communication.

If mutual communication is over, reciprocally everything is over.

Your success depends on the effect of your communication.

The quality of your communication is decided by you, and your identity is determined by the words you choose to speak. The politeness in our words makes our personality attractive and also makes us popular among people.

A sweet voice works like hypnotism. By it anybody can be influenced. By using polite speech and adopting a polite way of talking, one can please anyone.

With a sweet voice we can make friends even with strangers but with a cruel voice even our friends leave us.

The wounds of the weapons heal with time, but the wounds caused by harsh words do not heal even in a lifetime.

To present your talk without making an enemy is an art.

The meaning of an entire sentence changes if we use one wrong word, or give a pause at a wrong place. The style in which we talk matters a lot too.

People do not hear or agree with those persons who do not use their language or style of communication. It means for your communication to be effective you need to talk by considering the other person's language and status.

Use maximum eye contact while talking so that you can understand others' feelings.

If any topic needs to be repeated then you should always repeat it.

Use clear words to put across your intention and purpose.

Always use words of praise whenever possible, because everyone likes to be praised. To be praised is in the nature of humans.

During discussions always use formal words in between, such as sorry, thank you, excuse me, please, etc., as the atmosphere during discussions is usually official and orderly.

Own up to your mistakes. Do not blame others for it.

If you do not know a thing, say that you are not aware of it.

Useless chatter tires our brain and we lose energy. Talk short and sweet.

Keep discussions short. By prolonged discussions you are wasting your time as well as of others.

Always discuss what is wrong and what is right. Do not discuss who is wrong and who is right. Criticise the action, not the person.

Do not convert discussions into arguments. As long as it's a discussion things remain under control, but arguments turn ugly and people may go to any point to prove themselves right. Never try to prove the other person wrong. Even if he is wrong try to understand him. Instead of getting entangled in contradiction, change the topic. If possible reach an agreement rather than having an argument.

Never be angry; try to be quiet and patient during discussions.

Our body language indicates our acceptance, rejection, mental status, desire, disinclination, positive energy, the need for clarification, peace, disturbance, liberal approach, arrogance, feelings of security/insecurity, tendency to take decisions or postpone, difficulty, pleasure, etc. Keeping these in mind, our discussions become more effective, and our communication becomes the medium of success.

Silence is stronger than the words. Sometimes things left unsaid can be better put across using body language. Be it personal life or professional life, the nonverbal communications are very helpful and they should not be considered less important than verbal communication. Meaningful and effective teaching is one that is presented by behaviour and not by speech.

Truly the art of communication is the foundation of a relationship, and the conversation that occurs in the absence of this art becomes the reason for a breakup in a relationship. Hence, always take care of the language that you are using during your communication and always consider the status of the person with whom you are communicating for the communication to become effective.

As speech and communication opens up and people feel free to talk anything, the art of communicating has begun to deteriorate. Nowadays instead of talking people taunt each other; also age is not considered during a conversation. This has lead to an increased number of broken relationships – between husband and wife, between siblings, between parents and children, between boss and subordinate, etc.

Always talk in a manner so as to clarify misunderstanding.

Every day spend at least 20 minutes with your spouse, 15 minutes with your children, and 10 minutes with yourself; meet and interact with your neighbour once a week.

Try to communicate with the other person by becoming his age – become a child with children.

Always address your friends, colleagues, business associates, and customers by name.

Never rebuke the messenger.

Be a bearer of good news.

It is very important to know the right time to talk and the appropriate time to end a conversation.

Art of communication is not speaking the right thing at the right time; abstaining from saying the wrong thing despite having a strong urge to, is an even bigger art.

Be a good listener before being a good speaker. Try to listen to the other person calmly and question him only once he finishes his discussion. Do not try to interrupt when someone is talking.

Some words are used in a symbolic manner. These should be understood to be able to respond appropriately. Such symbolic language is used to avoid hurting the other person's feelings. For instance, if your boss asks, "Is your watch running fine?" he is actually trying to make you realise that you are late and should start reporting on time to office. Learn to read the face. The face is an indicator of the thoughts running in the mind. Whenever you write, write positive things and always read it once.

"We are sorry that you are in pain, but we are happy to know that you have given us an opportunity to help you by bringing this to our notice." Such simple messages work wonders.

Greet people over the phone with a happy voice. If the person you are calling is not present leave a message with your name and phone number so that he knows who called.

An intelligent person is one who can identify the better thing out of two good things and can identify the worst thing out of two bad things. If he is compelled to tell a bad thing then he should choose to tell the one that is less bad.

Science of Giving

The art of giving is also a science. It is important that we give and equally important is the manner in which we give. Giving should come from deep within the heart; it should be accompanied by genuine emotions, nobility and intimacy.

Sometimes it becomes very difficult for some friends and relatives to ask for favours. Try to understand their problems and necessities and contribute your help to them without being asked. The act of giving should be as discreet as possible. Never declare openly once you have helped others; this results if false pride. Also never show any obligation to the receiver. Help and give others in a manner that even they are not aware that it is you who is helping them. Try to be practical with your giving. Sometimes we go overboard with our gifts not realising that our loved ones should also find our gifts useful. For instance it is better to gift a fruit basket rather than an expensive box of sweets.

Another art of sharing and giving exists that makes you immortal. Life teaches all of us many lessons as we progress through life. When you share them with others and they adopt them in their lives then you become immortal. Hence, share your experiences of life with others. There is no cost of love, encouragement, respect, praise, happiness, and knowledge that you share with others. These are priceless gifts so give and share them as much as you can.

The store house of materials is obtained by collecting them but the store house of happiness, love, respect, peace, and knowledge is obtained by distributing them.

As You Give So You Receive

If you want to get love
then give love to others.
If you want to get kindness
then show mercy to others.
If you want to be respected
then first respect others.
If you want others to be tolerant,
then be tolerant towards them.
If you want others to praise you
then first praise others.
We cannot help ourselves
without helping others first.
We cannot benefit ourselves
without benefitting others first.
We cannot be prosperous,
without first making others prosperous.

According to the principle of deed and destiny — our deeds decide our destiny and the results thereon.

Ego (Pride)

Ego, or arrogance, is a major obstruction in life. It hampers progress and leads to drastic circumstances.

A person who boasts and pretends and tries to have people sing his praises is an egoist. Such people develop false pride that leads to their downfall in life. Pride is intoxicating; a proud person is always in search of people who will praise and flatter him. He thinks he is worthy of praise because he considers himself superior and others around him inferior. His ego gets a boost when others sing his praises and obey him, but when such things do not happen, he feels insulted and gets angry. Such people also tend to develop a feeling of jealousy towards others. They cannot stand to see people living happy and prosperous lives.

People having false pride and ego develop disaffection towards others, which leads to their isolation from society. They tend to develop evil thoughts and are also sometimes drawn towards wrong and immoral activities. These people fail to make true friends. They are attracted to people who shower them with false adorations and sing false praises; such selfish people who lie can never be true friends. When ego enters the head it brings about downfall in a person's life.

The pride of beauty, capability, status, and power cause failure and the person starts making mistakes. This destroys his intelligence, imagination, and farsightedness because of which he loses his acquaintances and may end up making more enemies than friends. He wastes his energies trying to defend himself against these enemies and brings about his own downfall. He begins to miss opportunities and loses his constructive approach.

Ego destroys the path of progress and development. It is only foolish people who think they know all; wise and learned people know that learning never ends. They know that knowledge is a big ocean of which they have tasted only a few drops. They understand that the more one gains knowledge the more one appreciates the fact that there is more to learn and become enlightened. Knowledge in a foolish person's hand is very risky, because for him a little knowledge is a dangerous thing.

If you want to be successful and prosperous, sacrifice your ego and give up your false pride. Ego obstructs the subconscious mind and makes you waste your positive energies in wrong pursuits. Renounce your ego and live a peaceful and satisfactory life.

Advice

Though the demand of advice is low, it is the one thing that is given the most.

A person who gives advice without being asked to and a person who refuses to take the advice are both fools. Avoid seeking advice from a person who has a selfish motto. Select a path that is judicious and balanced.

Advice should be accepted from a person who inspires you to think about yourself and encourages you to reach your goal in life.

Try to always take advice from intelligent people. There is no harm in accepting advice if it is beneficial and causes no harm.

Do consult others, but at the end the decision should always be your own. If you like the advice and think it is beneficial for you without any loss then there is no harm in accepting it.

As far as possible avoid giving advice to others without being asked to. The best time to give advice is when you are asked to.

A foolish person is obsessed to improve others, whereas an intelligent person is obsessed to improve himself.

Learn To Say No

It is very important to learn to say "no" when we want to. People around us always ask us to do something they are unable to do at that point of time or to help them out with something; life is such. Often people ask us to make promises that we may be uncomfortable or unable to keep. At times we may not have the time but because of our hesitation to say "no" we end up giving our word and suffer. It is good habit to help others but this can be practiced to a limit. If we remain busy trying to fulfil the needs and promises of others when will we find time for ourselves and our families. This is when it becomes to know when to say "no". The hint is: when you feel uncomfortable saying "yes" that is when you should be sure it is time you said "no".

Difficulty to say "no" will force you into being busy with other people's work. After some time you will not only become irritable and angry at yourself and others, but you will also destroy your relationships and bonds of friendships. In the long run such a situation will lead to tension and disturbance and may adversely affect your health too.

Some people who hesitate in saying "no" have the feeling that service is done by good people and to say "no" would mean they are selfish and rude.

A person who is in the habit of saying "yes" to everyone remains surrounded by unwanted and useless work, and rarely succeeds in completing any task satisfactorily and successfully. If you promise to complete some work and are not able to deliver it within the stipulated time, you will be labeled an irresponsible individual. It is better to say "no" in such a case.

Teach yourself to say "no" however difficult it is at first. Negative habits too are developed as a result of not being able to say "no" to the habit. Under peer pressure we start smoking, drinking, consuming drugs, etc., and then suffer when we are addicted to these harmful substances. Had we said "no" the first time, this would never have happened. Learn to say "no" to negative thoughts and "yes" to happiness and peace in your life.

Decide your priorities and then depending on these say "yes" or "no" to others. Successful people recognise their priorities and accordingly promise or commit. They never say "yes" against their will. You can politely turn down a request without hurting the other person. Be reasonable and sensible and make the other person see your view point. Never feel guilty after you have said "no" to someone. Some of the polite and courteous ways of saying a sweet "no" are:

"I can't help you at present"

"I can do this work next month"

"This is not possible for me at the moment"

"This is not possible in my busy schedule"

"At present I am busy with some other work"

"I don't think I am capable to do this work"

"I can't do this, but I can suggest a person who can" (apply this only when you know someone else)

Say "No, thanks" without bringing any harshness or dullness in your demeanour.

Public Speaking

Public speaking means addressing a large number of people. If the idea of speaking in front of a gathering makes you nervous and you are unable to present your speech properly, then you need to get rid of the fear of public speaking. To lessen the internal fear, take a deep breath and release it before you take the stage. Try to be normal and relaxed. Tell yourself: "I have the capability and I will do it." This will enhance your self-confidence and lessen your nervousness.

Pre-practice is another way of getting rid of your stage fright. At home stand in front of a mirror and practice speaking on different subjects, looking and observing your mirror image at all times.

Once you are ready and take the stage, stand at least 23 cm away from the mike and start speaking by keeping your head straight. Keep your hands free while speaking, and use them to gesture if needed. Try to look in all directions while speaking. It should not seem as if you are only speaking to a section of the group. Keep the tone and ascent–decent of your voice normal pace and according to the matter of the speech. To avoid your voice from breaking while speaking, drink a cup of hot water before the speech.

Try to use minimum words to clearly express your ideas and thoughts. Do not use complicated words to explain yourself. To properly use your time on the stage, avoid deviating from the topic of discussion. Many speakers waste their time only in the introduction and their time ends.

Make sure you have something important and informative to say during your speech. Focus on the topic of discussion while speaking, and be courteous and fair-spoken. Keep your speech interesting and acceptable; speak in a fashion that the audience does not get bored.

Don't forget to add examples, facts, and figures as per the requirement in your speech. Examples should match with the matter of your speech. Make sure that you do not use too many facts and figures or the speech will become boring and maybe too heavy to be understood all at once. Always prepare some general questions to ask the audience. If you keep the entire exercise interactive, the audience will be active in its participation as well as interested in the talk.

As a speaker you should refrain from criticising anybody while presenting your speech. Stick to the topic of discussion and try to make it fun and interesting as much as possible without joking personally about anyone.

Using small pauses between lines and after particular words while speaking create a dramatic effect.

Subject, language, and time are important factors in a speech. How a speaker put his points across and how well he displays his presentations also play an important role in making a speech a good one. Avoid using exaggerated and absurd gestures while speaking, as this may have an adverse effect on the audience. The speaker's facial expressions should help convey his message well and assist him in his speech. Have a happy face when talking about happy things or news; be serious when discussing sad things.

Try to finish your speech within the stipulated time. If time permits, repeat the main points of the speech in the end to sum up the entire talk. Conclude your speech on a climax to make it impressive and effective.

Even if the speaker is incapable, the mental support of a loveable and virtuous audience can boost his capabilities.

Art of Listening

Listening is an art. For this art we require both the ears and our concentration. Along with listening, speaking is also important. That is why it is natural that one who is dumb by birth is also deaf. This is because if he only listens and is unable to speak he will become mentally imbalanced.

When listening and speaking take place together it results in a conversation. When we participate we remember better. That is why you will notice that we can't remember speeches, because we were merely listening, but we don't forget conversations that we have had, because we have shared it with someone.

Nature has given us two ears and one mouth; taking a hint from nature, we should listen more and speak less.

Avoid listening to idle chatter and gossip. When we listen to nonsense, we tend to speak it too. Remember – garbage in, garbage out. Do not listen to things that will destroy your peace and happiness.

To become a good listener

1. Concentrate on the speaker. Maintain eye contact with the speaker. Reaction should be expressed by smiling or by nodding the head. For understanding something ask a question, but undue interruption should be avoided. Emphasis should not be on the words but understanding what the speaker is saying; the subject of the speaker is important.

2. Notice the expressions and emotions and not just the words. It is better to concentrate on the ascending and the descending voice of the speaker.
3. Avoid come up with a conclusion about a conversation in a hurry; take time to think about it and then judge

A good listener is not only liked and admired by everybody, he is also able to learn a lot by listening patiently to others' points of view.

Body Language

Gestures and postures interpret what is going on in one's mind. Body language tells a lot about the personality of a person.

The personality of a person is the mirror of his thinking and behaviour. A person is identified by his personality, his manner of working, his approach to different circumstances, his bodily gestures and postures, etc. Just as personality can make a person seem dignified, in the same way it can make him infamous. The personality of a person is judged first by his body's gestures and postures.

When you meet someone for thc first time, the first impression presented by you becomes posted in the other person's mind. Before you even talk, your body language creates a mark. That is why it is important to maintain a good body language.

Wherever you go, whatever you do — at the market, in the office, during an interview — a good body language helps you present a positive personality to the person in front of you. It is interesting to know and observe the body language from time to time because it is the best and trustworthy way to judge a person quickly.

A person's speech, behaviour, and actions interpret his mental status and possible conduct.

An intellectual person can catch such indications that others cannot.

A lot of questions get answered by noticing the body language of the other person. For instance, while talking to your boss or asking him questions, if you observe carefully you can get the answers to most of your questions by his body language.

The capability of reacting in a particular manner under certain circumstances can be developed naturally, if we are able to master the skill of reading the body language of others.

Train yourself to be more aware of not only the other person's body language but also your own.

A hand shake says it all

The shaking of hands in greeting says a lot about another person. When a person shakes both hands instead of one hand, it means he is courteous towards you and wants to be friendly to you.

If the palm of the hand is towards the left, it indicates that the other person considers you of the same level. If he bows a bit it means that the other person honours you in the level of seniority.

During a hand shake, if a person keeps his palm turned towards the upper side it indicates that he is calm and gentle and wants to make friendship with you.

If the palm is facing downwards it indicates that the person wants to dominate you. Such people are dictators by nature.

If a person shakes the hand for a longer period then he is expressing his happiness after meeting you.

If a person snatches his hand away at once after the hand shake it means he is not very much interested in being friends.

Sometimes we experience cold soft hands during a hand shake. People with such a hand shake are unenthusiastic and weak.

Some people press the hands very hard during a hand shake; such people try to express their power.

Ladies frequently change their style of hand shake according to the circumstances. If they want to express their sympathy, they just hold both hands gently rather than shaking the hand. If they just put their fingers forward for a hand shake it shows the presence of insecurity in them.

What a face speaks

During a conversation if the face of the speaker is aligned with the listener, it means the person is aware and alert.

If the face of the speaker is bent towards you, it means he is surprised by your conversation, is listening intently, and is finding it interesting.

If a person is bored by your talks or is already aware of the things you are speaking then his face will be a bit backwards.

During a conversation if somebody all of a sudden covers his face by his hands it means something unwanted has been said by him that he wanted to hide.

If a person bends his face in a particular direction then it means that some particular plan is going on in his mind or he is getting emotional.

A sweet smile expresses respect and interest. An ugly face gesture shows annoyance.

A distressed face shows difficulty.

An asymmetrical face shows fraudulence.

What the eyes speak

An eye-to-eye contact with the speaker or listener shows self-confidence.

If someone changes his eye direction during a conversation it shows that he is hiding something.

If a person makes eye contact at the start of a conversation but starts avoiding eye contact gradually, it means that he is losing interest in the conversation.

A steady look means respect.

Open wide eyes show happiness.

Shrinking of eyes expresses objection.

The rapid blinking of eyes expresses a difficult situation.

What the head speaks

If the head is straight while talking, it means that the speaker is adamant.

Bowing the head a bit shows respect.

Moving the head up and down shows interest or consent.

Moving the head left to right shows disagreement or objection.

Moving the head slowly from side to side means that the person is despaired and is going through difficulties. Moving the head up and down while saying "no" or moving the head from left to right while saying "yes" shows fraudulence.

Posture

The posture can speak a lot about a person. If a person crosses his arms and places them in front of his chest, then the person is being defensive and trying to maintain a distance from the other person.

If a person is sitting with his hand on his cheek it means he is thinking.

A person is influencing and showing his dominance if he folds his hands at the back.

Looking at the watch after every short interval shows that the person is in a hurry.

A person is bored if he is sitting with one leg on the other.

The slow rubbing or touching of nose shows that the person is in a position of doubt.

If a person hits his head with his hands while working, it shows that he has committed a mistake.

If the speaker rubs the edges of his eyes, it indicates that he is either telling a lie or is diverting the other's attention.

In a false laugh only the mouth is used, while in a natural laugh both the mouth and the eyes respond together.

Saluting with the palm showing marks respect; saluting with the back of the palm showing means ego and false pride.

Precautions

1. Body language differs from person to person and situation to situation. Same indications at different times convey different meanings. Scratching head could mean a perspiring head, a head full of lice,

forgetting something, telling a lie, or uncertainty; it could be anything.

2. Context and circumstances of conversation should also be considered while observing the body language. Folding of hands, arms, and legs tightly during winter indicates that a person is feeling cold; here he is not trying to be defensive.
3. It is important to know and consider the matter on which one is speaking before judging the body language.
4. If what a person is speaking is different from his body language, then rely on the body language.
5. If a man speaks in a manner that is different from his body language, then such a man is either neglected or ignored by women.

People who lie or hide facts do not make eye contact. They will either scratch something with their hands or legs or will start biting their nails.

When people are nervous

They crack their fingers, put hands on their head repeatedly, or tighten their hands into fists.

Restless people

Play with their hair, shake their legs while sitting, or unnecessarily touch parts of their body.

Confident people

Sit straight, keep the position of their shoulders erect while sitting, keep chest out and erect, occupy the full chair, keep their neck straight, maintain eye contact while talking, walk fast and straight, and smile.

A Successful Manager

The success or failure of a manager does not depend on what he does or how much of a task he does, but depends on how capable he is in getting the work done from others.

A successful manager always keep in mind the benefits of his employees and their families from the time they begin working for him. He knows that an employee can put in his maximum efforts only when he feels safe and satisfied. Such managers can get brilliant work done even from their less skilled worker.

A successful manager always thanks his colleagues and subordinates for their co-operation. The act of thanking people brings them close to him. Other than this, by apologising for his wrong behaviour and talks, he controls any controversies and negative feelings against him.

A successful manager never needs to pressurise his subordinates to work; he merely motivates them and they work.

His main emphasis is customer satisfaction and excellence in work. An efficient manager also contributes to an improvement in production and is responsible for the profits earned by his company.

Some other qualities of a good manager are

1. A positive attitude
2. Polite and clear articulation
3. Self-guided and driven
4. A goal setter
5. Bold

6. Responsible and reliable
7. Punctual
8. Patient and cool headed
9. A good listener
10. Team oriented

Job Interview

An interview is the first step of your career. It is on the basis of an interview that it is decided whether you are selected or rejected. That is why it is important that you should answer all questions intelligently and smartly.

Before going for the interview try and understand the work culture and attitude of the company. If you know someone in the company, ask them about the organisation and its functioning. An interview is that examination in which even a small mistake can ruin all your hard work and efforts. That is why during an interview speak only what is required and when it is required.

You have only some time in which you are required to give many details. Proper time management skills can aid you in providing equal time to all subjects. Your aim should be to utilise your time to the maximum, and in any circumstance don't talk on useless points.

When you are asked about your expected salary, do not hesitate or avoid talking about it. You have to mention your minimum expectation. Think honestly that whether you are capable of what you have asked for.

Never bad mouth your previous company, if you have worked in one. Do not lie about your last salary in your previous job. Talk only within your limits.

Make sure that when you are asked about your future career plans, you include the "interview company" in your plans. It is obvious that the interviewer will want to know how in future you will be adjusting and working for the company.

Always show your eagerness to learn. Most companies provide jobs to people who are eager to learn and upgrade their skills.

Never ask what your company will provide you; try to see what you can do for the company and what will be your contribution to the company.

Body language during an interview

Holding a proper posture and displaying appropriate gestures in an interview are more important than answering all the questions. This is because the interviewer's impression of you is judged a lot by your body language. A soft smile and a proper expression can enrich your personality.

During an interview the following things should be kept in mind

Sit comfortably and place both your feet on the floor; avoid placing one leg upon the other.

Do not sit with your arms folded in front of you. This signals that you are being defensive.

Maintain eye contact while talking. This shows you are confident.

If there is more than one person interviewing you, make eye contact with the person who is talking to you and not with the others at that point of time.

Move your eyes from one person to another while talking so that it looks like you are talking to all of them.

Speak in a clear and disciplinary manner. Change your tone when it is necessary and avoid uniformity.

Give a pause before speaking. There are chances you will make mistakes if you try to answer instantly.

Talk a bit softer than your normal voice.

Don't talk too loudly or too slowly.

Don't get excited on any point of disagreement.

Don't put your hands on your face while speaking.

Your voice should reflect enthusiasm and eagerness. Bowing yourself, keeping your hands free, moving your head in consent – such type of actions show your responsibility and eagerness.

Make Your Employees The Best

Motivate your employee to be customer oriented.
Develop the habit of co-operation in your employees.
If an employee makes a mistake motivate him to learn from that mistake and proceed further.
Try to engage the mind of your employees.
Improve the efficiency of the employees through training.
Solve the problems of your employees whenever you can.
Try to delegate work of interest to the workers.
Inspire your employees to think.
Delegate work to your employees but don't forget.
Maintain the self-respect of your employees.
Develop good time management skills. Value and manage the time of your employees and yours, like money.
Develop coordination with and among your employees.
Motivate your employees to present their suggestions.
Act cautiously with some crooked employees.

Teach your employees:

To say "thanks" and "sorry" instantly;
to learn from criticism;
to learn to control anger;
to be honest.

Give motivational rewards to employees from time to time for their good work.

Impart training to the employees from time to time whenever required so that their skills improve.

For example, in a retail business, employees should be taught artistic ways of influencing customers, the art of effective communication, and the skill of judging customers. Imparting special training to employees in a specific field makes them strong and confident in that field.

Importance of Remembering Names

Make a habit of remembering names. If you do so the other person will feel that you are interested in him.

The capability of remembering names is important in business, social contacts, and politics.

People are so proud of their name that they try to maintain its existence at any cost. The name of a person is the sweetest and the most important thing for him.

That is why people write their names on structures, monuments, etc.

To make people close to you, it is important you remember their names to make them feel important. This is very easy, how many of us actually practice is what is worth noticing.

Many people are not able to remember names. This is because they do not make any effort to memorise others' names with concentration. To be able to remember and reproduce someone's name one has to try and memorise in a manner that the name creates a mark in their mind. Many times we meet strangers and strike a friendship with them. During that brief time that we are friends, we spend more than half the time gossiping with them and depart without remembering their names.

Never make the mistake of writing or saying someone's name incorrectly.

To be successful at whatever you do, make it a habit of addressing your friends, colleagues, business associates, and customers with their names.

Accept The Changes

Change is a rule of nature. Change is the only inevitable thing.

This era is of science and technology. In such times changes are happening very fast. Changes that have taken place in the last one hundred and fifty years have changed the world's way of living. Now more changes are taking place than ever before. The world is truly going through a wave of changes.

Every person goes through some change or another, whether he likes it or is ready for it or not.

Usually the changes in our lives are not instant. That is why we must keep an eye on the going ons in our lives and be ready to do what needs to be done at the time of change. Big changes can be avoided or handled better by observing small changes; these changes can help us adjust ourselves to certain difficult situations. Once you have accepted change, it is important that you change fast, because if you do not mould yourself in time according to the new situation then possibly it will be of no use later.

People who search for new destinations even before reaching the upper limits of change are the ones who attain main heights and can fly their victory flags and also search for newer and higher destinations.

Some people are in the habit of always opposing change, even if they can benefit from it. They forever want to avoid changes.

Avoiding changes is not the solution because then the problems only increase instead of decreasing. If you do not change according to the situation, then in the times to come you will surely be ruined.

This anecdote explains change the best. As we are aware, Chinese people eat frog. Previously they use to boil the water and then put the frog into it, but the frog would jump out of the water because of the water's heat. Then the Chinese decided to change the way of cooking the frog. Now they put the frog in normal water and let the frog swim, and then they slowly start warming the water on a low flame. The amazing thing is that the frog continues to swim and remains unaware of the water getting heated and gets cooked. Do you know the reason for this? The reason is that the frog moulds with the gradually increasing heat and by the time it realises the grave situation it is in, it is too late.

If we do not recognise the changing situations in our lives in time then we too may be destructed like the frog. That is why it is very important that regular and good changes are done for better development and progress.

Successful people accept change as normal and a part of life. Your being simple and normal becomes a special quality if it is accompanied by some positive change. Be gentle but do not lose opportunities just because change is a part of it. Changes are the demand of today's times. If you don't change, time and people around you will change and you will be left behind. It is better to accept change and adapt accordingly, rather than repent later in life. It is not sensible to sit idle after attaining new height. Keep on seeking new options because this change is not the last change. Hence, be prepared for the next change. Every start has an end, and every end has a start.

If we do not change according to the changes, we will get ruined. If we change according to the changes, we will manage to exist. Prosperity will be ours if we accept change and start changing.

Turn Your Arranged Marriage Into A Love Marriage

In a love marriage, we love first and then get married whereas in an arranged marriage, first marriage happens then love. Love in an arrange marriage develops slowly only once we know and understand each other. According to analysts, arranged marriages are more stable than love marriages.

In a love marriage, love dominates the heart and brain, so much so that we can see only the positive qualities of each other. But after the marriage when one faces the problems of family life, the love gradually begins to diminish and intimacy decreases between the couple. Love and faith are the foundation of a marriage; they should be allowed to develop slowly. A relation develops gradually when you sprinkle it with your positive behaviour and lots of patience.

In arranged marriages the general tradition is to match the horoscope of the girl and boy. The horoscope, it is believed, shows their destiny; though this practice is changing nowadays. Destiny is a result of our old actions that cannot be changed. Our present actions and destiny decides our future. Hence, instead of matching the horoscopes the following precautions can be followed so that the life of the couple is full of togetherness and doesn't become a burden.

Select your priorities

Decide what you are and what are your demands and likings. On the basis of these priorities you can decide the kind of partner you would like. For example, is it education that is important to you or looks? Should your partner be modern or traditional? Do you prefer a joint family or a nuclear one? Do you prefer a working wife or a housewife? Once these priorities are set you can begin the search for your partner.

Compromise is important but...

Most people desire a partner who is the most talented and has all the ideal qualities that a partner should have. But, in reality it is impossible to find such a person.

Make a list of the requirements that you would like in your partner. Then decide on which qualities you can compromise and on which you cannot. If you keep searching for a person who will meet all the requirements then you will remain a bachelor for life.

Concentrate on family

At the time of selecting a partner, it is common for people to think that the family doesn't matter, because it is the boy and girl who have to live together. But the truth is that marriage is not just a relationship between two people but it is between two families. So before arranging a marriage it is important to see the parents and close relatives of both the sides. Their behaviour will reflect the behaviour of the girl or boy. This is more important for the girl because she has to live in that house.

Look for similarity in families

Though it is said that in a marriage caste, religion, area, age, background, etc., do not matter, but in reality they do matter. If one lives in a nuclear family these differences do not matter as much, but if one lives in a joint family then these differences can bring bitterness in your relations. For example, if you are a vegetarian and have married into a non-vegetarian family, you may face difficulty to adjust in the relationship. In the same way if your upbringing has been traditional, do not look for a modern girl or for external glamour. On the same lines, family, career, business, etc., can be considered.

Match the values in your partner

It is common belief that if the likes and dislikes of a girl and a boy match then they are fit for each other. However, similar hobbies and habits do not hold much importance in the long run. What is important is that both the partners should have similar basic value systems and thinking. For example, if one likes to go to the pub and disco and other prefers to go to the temple, then this is a major difference.

Look for complementary qualities

Families believe that in a perfect relation it is best that the boy and girl have common shortcomings. But, this is a wrong approach, because marriage means a bond in which each partner tries to complete the other. It is good that one knows how to cook food and the other does not. If one is short-tempered the other should be peaceful by nature. That is why look for complementary qualities of your behaviour.

Don't ignore nature

Generally the nature and character of the boy and girl are not given much importance while choosing a partner. The girl and boy should try to find out how much loving, sacrificing, and supportive the other person is. Will they support unconditionally or not and other such behaviour patterns. People do not emphasise on communication skills, which is also very important for a good and successful relationship.

Look at yourself

Every person has some specialities and some drawbacks. We should focus on our drawbacks rather than expect all the specialities from the other person. See your drawbacks and your defects. Don't be artificial, and don't only praise yourself but mention your drawbacks too. If you mention your shortcomings your partner will not have high expectations in future. Keep your mind clear that marriage doesn't only mean to achieve something, but it also means to be prepared to give love, honour, and care to your partner for life. Prepare yourself to take responsibilities. Your partner may be perfect, but the relationship will not be successful if you are not prepared to be a responsible partner in the relationship.

Ask questions frankly

Girls and boys avoid many important questions when they meet. Girls generally keep quiet as they think the others will feel bad and disrespected. The two families try to speak as less as possible to each other, because the more they talk, the more weakness will be apparent. This is an incorrect way of going about such things.

How can they find out about each other without communicating? In fact, it is sensible to ask and tell each other things clearly so that later in the relationship problems do not crop up. Create a relationship based on truth; this will lead to less problems in the future. Of course, questions should be asked in such a manner that the other person doesn't feel bad. At the same time it is important to know how much truth is there in the other's talk. For this it is good to talk about the past rather than about the future. This will aid in knowing the reality of the other person.

Keep in mind the following

There should not be much difference in the financial status of the two families. If the girl is from a very rich family then she will have special lifestyle habits, without which she will not be able to adjust in life.

If there is vast difference in education, then it is very difficult to maintain mental coordination.

A big difference in age can also create problems afterwards.

It is important that the boy is self-dependent.

For a happy married life, the bride and groom should take an oath that if sometime I am on fire, you become water and if at times you become fire then I will become the stream of water.

Family Planning

Population explosion has been our country's biggest problem for years now. The only way to control this problem is the adoption of family planning measures.

An increase in population means an increase in the number of newborns. But an increase in newborns means deterioration in the health of the mother, the fall in the economic status of the father, and slowness in the progress and development of the country. With so many problems, the future of the newborns too is handicapped. The continuous increase in population has lead to a shortage of survival resources and a reduction in the development programmes for children.

The proper development of a family happens when the children develop properly. Proper development of children is possible when parents have families that are big enough for them to properly and efficiently take care of. For children to develop and grow properly, each child should be fed, clothed, and educated in a manner that makes them healthy, fit, and literate. There should be overall development of the child and this is possible if the number of children in each family is controlled. A large family loses its comforts and struggles to meet its everyday needs. Parents and children suffer and living becomes a burden.

Small families live better and secure lives. A single child gets more attention, more quality time, and so obviously is more successful in life. The parents have more resources to use and spend on his overall development and that is why he becomes more efficient at whatever he does. He also grows up to be a self-confident individual.

For proper economical, social, family and personal comforts, the first child in a family should be healthy, smart, and born at the right age. The aim of every parent should be in having a small and organised family.

Development of Children

It is the moral responsibility of parents to bring up their child properly and educate and make them self-dependent.

Till the time a married couple does not have a child they are desperate to have one, and they do everything they can to become parents. But once they manage to become parents they become indifferent towards those things that are necessary for the perfect development of their children.

Sometimes parents, by their detrimental and insignificant love, make their children lazy, amorous, gluttonous, egoistic, naughty, and faulty. For the overall development of a child, it is important to encourage him at the right time and to punish him at the right time according to his mistake.

Always remember that a newly born child learns regularly from our conduct and behaviour. At this early age, whatever he is taught becomes a base for development of his nature and his future is moulded in the same manner. For people who understand these facts, it becomes their moral responsibility to keep a control on their immoral behaviours and be ready to sacrifice anything to maintain a calm and pleasant atmosphere at home. For the sake for their children they should be happily ready for this.

True learning in children happens not from the learning at school but from the examples set by their elders. Their undeveloped brain is unable to understand lengthy and strict instructions, but they are better equipped at understanding and following things that happen around them. That is why we should present things in front of children in a way from which they can learn. Children don't do what they are asked to do but instead they do what they see us doing.

Until we ourselves follow a good character, respect our elders (parents, teachers, and other aged people), follow a disciplined life, live together in a family and with neighbours, help the poor, helpless, and handicapped, follow moral duties, protect the morals and limits of our own sisters and daughters as well as others' sisters and daughters, till then we cannot expect our children to follow and do these good acts.

Every parent expects their children to grow up in a good manner, but to bring up children in a good or bad manner depends on how the parents nurture them.

Parents need to nurture their children with complete interest and responsibility so that they develop in a positive manner.

As craftsmen and potters carve stone and shape raw mud to create beautiful toys, statues, and different types of utensils, in the same way parents can make their children brave, timid, or great personalities by their loving care and good nurturing.

History shows how the great personalities were nurtured and raised; the credit goes to their mothers for making them eminent.

In some families the fathers maintain a distance from their children though physically they are very near. Such fathers hurt the tender mind of their children by adopting this tough exterior and strict behaviour.

For the emotional growth of a child, it is very important that the spirit of security arises in his mind. Hence, parents should have the knowledge of emotions and accordingly nurture their children.

If a child gets complete love during his childhood, then in future he shares it with his classmates and friends. But, if he himself is deprived of love, then it is impossible for him to share it with others.

Generally parents nowadays are busy earning a living and creating resources for their children. They are forced to leave aside their duties of developing a good character of their children. When these children grow up, they uselessly spend all their wealth and get into bad company. Thus, it is of utmost importance that children should be developed and made well cultured from the very beginning.

Children are the most valuable priorities of our life. To look after them and maintain a good atmosphere for them should be our topmost priority and responsibility. To shape their personalities is a unique and creative job. For this, extended care and guidance is required.

Before expecting the child to understand us, we should ourselves try to understand the child. (For detailed information read author's book 'Development of Children').

Eggs break in two ways – one, when we break them and two, when they break on their own. When we break an egg, there is no existence of this unnaturally broken egg and later we eat it by using it to make an omelette or egg curry. But when it breaks naturally, a chicken comes out of it and there is a creation of new life. In the same way when we stop a child from working according to his will or choice and compel him to do things according to the way we want him to, the result is the same as breaking the egg by force. But when we allow the child to work according to his will then his talent is enhanced, his personality brightens, and he gains self-confidence. So, guide your children but do not force them into doing things they have no curiosity for.

Girl Child – Curse or Blessing

In our country the love for a boy child is very common. A lot of people do not want to accept girls as their children. If these people are blessed with only girls and no boy child then they feel their house is deserted and their future is dark without a boy. If our body is not ours, how can a son be ours?

All this exists because of our mindsets that have not changed for generations. One person is satisfied and happy if he has no child or if he has only one girl child. On the other hand another person thinks having a girl child is a curse and so he always remains unhappy and slowly loses his mental balance. This difference between the two men has no specific reason, but it is only a difference of the level of thinking. If the unhappy person changes his ideology to that of the satisfied person, then his grief and pain can easily be changed to happiness and satisfaction in just a moment. But the question is how many of us are willing to give up our obsession with the male child?

A father should feel blessed if he has only girl children; he should feel fortunate. After the marriage of his girl, a father is free from all responsibilities. Also the love for girls is more natural than in boys; there is no struggle with them for self-interest and thus no alienation. Selfless service is achieved when we bring up a girl child. After getting released from the daughter's responsibilities, the parents are free to devote their time, money, and minds in spirituality and self-improvement and can attain their ultimate goals and destiny of life. So, sensible and intelligent people remain satisfied by considering the girl child as a blessing of God. Therefore, if God has blessed us with a girl child, nourish her as a small plant and bring her up happily. Pratibha Patil, Kiran

Bedi, Sania Mirza, M. C. Marykom are all girls who made their parents and families proud. Then why this difference between girls and boys?

Daughters support their parents in all kinds of problems. Then why are only sons supposed to be the support of old age? Be it studies, board exams, or any other competitive exam, girls have been topping for years now, then why are boys still desired? But, there are still many people who do not want a girl child at all. To avoid giving birth to a girl child, people do abominable sins by opting for female foeticide.

If this situation continues then the fateful day is not far when girls will not be available for marriage with boys and the boys will be forced to spend their lives as bachelors. Absence of farsightedness has developed a vision in which boys are felt to be superior and girls inferior.

Our daughters go to other's house as the bride; in the same way other's daughters come to our house as the new bride. Daughters are given a farewell on one hand and on the other hand we welcome and accept girls from other's house as the new bride. In fact, the level of a daughter is high in all respects. Usually as soon as the sons start earning they leave the house. Sometimes they go away for higher education or for business reasons. Some of them leave their parents alone once they get married and begin a new life with their wives. It is rare that they help their family for education, marriage of their younger brother and sisters. They take over the business of their father and make them dependent on them even for a single penny. This is found in most of the families that have sons.

Women who differentiate between the male and the girl child should remember their self-esteem. They should realise their duties towards their children and not differentiate between girls and boys. They should treat both the girl and the boy with the same importance, same love, same interest, and affection. Both children are entitled to the love, care, and upbringing. Though girls who are supposed to be soft and tender, are becoming the biggest support and faith for their elderly parents today.

This is best described by the following proverb – A son is a son till he gets married, but a daughter remains a daughter till she is alive.

The Importance of Parents

Parents occupy a position even higher than God. God gives us both pleasure and pain but parents always try to give us happiness.

Of the two, the mother has got the highest place amongst all the teachers. A mother is the first teacher to her children. There is no example of sacrifice and affection like that of a mother in the world.

Parents play a very important role in the development of their children, both physically as well as temperamentally. They nurture their children and make them independent. This is what makes the children successful in their life. Not only do parents care for their children, but they also pray for their welfare and health.

Everything that we are today is because of our parents. They helped us walk and talk. We held on to their fingers and gained the confidence to take our first step. We are provided the best of education by our parents. Even in times of distress, parents always focus on their children first and make sure they are provided all the basic needs.

But when it is our turn to look after them in their old age, they are usually left alone and isolated to fend for themselves. The same parents who remain with us from our childhood to our youth and fulfil all our needs – big and tiny – are left all by themselves to manage on their own in their old age. Why does this happen? What crime have they committed? Is it fair to deprive them of our love and support at such a time in their life? Is it right for us to leave them empty handed at the end of their lives, when all their lives they have struggled to earn a living and provide us all the comforts and luxuries of life? The same fingers that we held on to for life as toddlers are again waiting to be held on to, but do we have the time or willingness to do so? If we don't ask ourselves these questions we will never realise the sin that we are committing. Imagine yourself in old age and your children not caring for you. Would you be happy?

Children need to realise that this is a cycle of love and sacrifice that will also guide their own children to look after them in their old age. Families in which elders are respected and honoured are the luckiest families.

It is the duty of the children to create a healthy and loving family atmosphere for their aged parents, just as their parents had created for them in their childhood.

A little bit of love and care and some precautions can make elders live a safe and healthy life in a way that they can freely enjoy their old age.

Some people who are unable to take care of their old parents, try to fulfil their needs financially. What we need to ask ourselves is, do the elderly need money or love, care, and assistance? There may be reasons why some children are compelled to stay away from their parents or can't keep their parents with them, but what they need to realise is that their parents need them. Generally all parents make compromises for their children, then why can't the children compromise for their aged parents?

We have to learn and teach ourselves to live together as a family with our parents. In some families the aged parents are more of a support than a liability. They extend their help in day-to-day work and look after their grandchildren. Such a family where all live by supporting each other is a happy family.

In some families there is token respect shown to old parents and grandparents. The children are not allowed near their grandparents, because of which no love and respect grows. What such families fail to see is that grandparents would like to mingle with their grandchildren, and both will benefit from such company of each other. If the children are a bit grown up then they help their grandparents with their work, and if the children are small then they make their grandparents do their work for them. A loving bond forms between the children and the grandparents and the grandparents live more active lives. If you really want your aged parents to lead healthy lives and want to care for them then don't deprive them of the wonderful world of grandchildren.

Once we are all big and grown up, we begin to find our parents boring and irritating. What we forget is that their current situation is so because for years they have been bearing our expenditures, washing our clothes, arranging our scattered things, collecting our favourite things, looking after us when we are sick, doing all our work including listening to us. That is why before reaching a conclusion about them, first think about yourself and how much you are responsible for their present situation.

In earlier times the elders were respected as the guardian deity of the house. They were respected for their experience, qualities, and efficiency. But as time passed, certain changes in behaviour took place and the elderly began to be ignored. They began to be mistreated and isolated. Some were thrown out of their houses, while some were sent to old age homes to die. But the universal truth is that sooner or later we too will be there someday, in the same situation and in the same condition. Let's never forget that.

Old age is the law of nature. Nobody remains young forever. As you behave with your children today, so will they behave with you in your old age. By being kind to your parents you are teaching your children to be kind to you. Remember: as you sow, so shall you reap.

There is a provision in the "Maintenance and welfare of parents and senior citizens bill 2007" that says that if children don't take care of their old parents, do not fulfil their daily needs, or misbehave with them, then they are bound to be punished by imprisonment and fine.

Relationships

A relationship is formed among people because of their connection by blood, or a relationship results between two people either when they develop an affinity for each other or when they get married.

Relationships can be maintained well if each member fulfils their responsibilities without bothering whether others are doing anything for them. This is the one very important principle that we should follow to maintain peace and harmony in our relationships. The key is to carry out your own duties without imposing yourselves on others or expecting anything in return from them. When expectations are low, you do not get hurt too often. You begin to believe – if it happens well and good and if it does not happen even then it is alright.

Most Indian families believe that they should continue doing their work without imposing their rights on others and without finding faults with others. When a family lives together by sacrificing for others and tries to work towards a common goal or interest then one person's pain becomes the pain of the entire family and similarly one person's success is shared equally by all members of the family. The entire family progresses together as well as faces tough times together. Such families bring happiness and prosperity to each other and life becomes a joyful journey than a burden.

All of us go through feelings of intimacy, affection, mutual love and care, happiness, sorrows, and discomforts. Over time we develop mutual faith, complement each other, and enjoy the spirit of service. As the relationship deepens we become sensitive towards each other and are able to feel each other's pain. Feeling of kinship between the members of a family is the best quality for the durability of a family.

Expression of faith and respect for elders, and the sharing of love and affection for the youngsters is the backbone of peace and prosperity in any family. To further strengthen family ties, try and fix a place at home where everybody can worship together.

Always insist on discussions rather than letting arguments happen. Arguments create misunderstandings. A healthy discussion happens when each family member appreciate the suggestions of the other members. Discuss every sorrow and happiness with each other, so that a strong bond develops between each other. If there are any misunderstandings, speak about them openly instead of hiding them; if you feel strongly about something never hesitate to discuss it freely with everyone. Nobody should be forced to do or say anything against their will. It is our duty towards each other to give space and freedom to each others' preferences. It is essential to praise members of the family on specific occasions and congratulate them on their success or motivate them to convert failure to success. This responsibility can be given to any elder of the family.

Bitterness in relationships

Misunderstandings in relationships destroy the bond that the partners share and faith is lost. No relationship can last for a long time without faith. When intimacy ends in close relationships then mutual love is shattered to pieces.

Allegations, criticisms, jealousy, hatred, etc., bring bitterness in relationships. Such negativities make people misbehave, their expectations from each other increases, they do not fulfil their responsibilities, they impose their likes and dislikes on others; in short, the family collapses like a pack of cards.

Improve your relationships

No relationship can continue to be the same forever. If at first there is intimacy then over time inconsistencies develop in the relationship and if at first their disagreement then with time intimacy develops. That is why never be rude to a person you do not get along with at present; you may regret your inappropriate behaviour later when the two of you befriend each other. Also try and save people you do not get along with from being insulted. Don't think about their defects. Don't disgrace their qualities. When you continue to respect their qualities, their stand for you changes and they may soften their approach towards you. With time and patience you will manage to win them over to your side. Try and understand people before you expect them to understand you. Communication is important. Even if the differences are huge, discussions should be continued. Don't let differences in opinion create differences in the heart.

Try to listen to each other, rather than dominating the conversation.

It is better to keep quiet when somebody is angry or upset, even if the other person seems to be wrong at that time. During arguments a silent language is much stronger than words. Once things have settled try to present your opinion calmly and appropriately. Never hesitate to share your feelings and opinions.

Before you try to change others, try to first change yourself. All of us have positive as well as negative qualities. It is better to understand and accept one's own weaknesses rather than exposing the weaknesses of others.

Never allow external disagreements and commotions to enter your house and shatter the peace within; similarly do not let family discords escape out of the boundaries of your house. Sometimes family disagreements extend to such a limit that brothers living together decide to live separately from each other. This may look like the only solution to bring peace in the family, but a person who tries to improve relationships instead of situations is the one who is sensible and dignified. A dead person is stiff; if we call ourselves alive then we also have to learn to be flexible and not rigid. All that is needed is a change in our attitudes. Instead of focusing on the negativities in our relationships, we have to merely overlook the deficiencies and adjust our attention on the good.

Consider the mother-in-law as a well-wisher not as an enemy

Due to the prevalence of some preconceived ideas and concepts in our society about mothers-in-law, they have come to be feared and at times hated by us. What we fail to understand is that she too is human and is merely being protective and at times possessive about her child, who she has raised. All that is needed is a change in attitude towards her.

Maintain a friendly relationship with her and give her all the attention she deserves. Avoid hiding information from her, and praise her for things she does for you. Build a relationship with her that is more of a friend. Share your thoughts and ideas with her and when she makes you understand about some things, try to learn and adopt some of her ideas.

Never try to ruin the relationship between your spouse and their mother. Give both of them importance and maintain a balance between the two. Never criticise either of them in front of each other. No child likes ill being spoken about their parent, and no mother can stand to see her child being rebuked and shouted upon.

Consider daughters-in-law as your own and not as outsiders

A daughter-in-law is the foundation of your future generation. Hence, she should get the same respect that is given to her husband. She deserves the same identity and her opinions should be given the same importance as are her husband's.

Daughters-in-law should get love and attention so that they have no difficulty adjusting to their new surroundings and family. When daughters-in-law are mistreated in front of their children, they develop wrong impressions in their young and immature minds, and get disturbed and confused to see their mother distressed. If not for anybody else, but for your grand children, stop torturing your daughters-in-law.

The husband too should maintain a balance in his relationship between his mother and his wife. Just as his mother is important to him, so is his wife. She is his future now and so her feelings and difficulties should be respected. The secret of happiness is to understand the position of both the mother and the wife and handle them accordingly.

Husband-Wife

The relationship between a husband and wife is not that of blood, but their relation is regarded more than blood relation. There is love, dedication, and faith in this relationship. The thread of this relationship is very delicate, and it should be held on to strongly.

Problems in a marriage start when the partners fail to understand each other. Over the years they may have developed a physical attraction and bond that they may enjoy but for a marriage to last and grow what is also needed is mutual understanding and respect for each other.

Couples usually enter a marriage painting a rosy picture about each other, thinking they are perfect. What they miss out is that nobody is perfect. We all have our many good qualities and some weaknesses. After marriage it is better to first try and understand each other, compromise on each other's weaknesses, and pay attention to each other's likings and daily habits. A lot of work, love, and understanding goes into making a marriage a success.

Things that are out of control should be accepted open heartedly, instead of resisting them. Avoid forcing your spouse into anything, be it a bad habit that has to be given up or some plan that is long overdue. Instead work on it with patience and a calm mind. Devote some "us" time to each other from your hectic schedules and take time to appreciate each other and take interest in each other's likings, hobbies, etc. Appreciation is a great weapon that can be used to make any situation favourable. Appreciation manages to bring out the good in every person. Appreciate family members rather than complaining about them in front of your spouse. Not only will they love you for this, but will also stand by you at the time of need.

Avoid complaining and accusing each other for the state of your marriage or family. Help each other in everyday tasks. Divide your duties and responsibilities sensibly so that both of you are carrying an equal burden. Appreciate each other for the good work done and motivate each other at times of failure and difficulties. Become each other's pillar of strength.

It is very important that husband and wife take out some quality time only for themselves every week. They should sit together and talk to each other about everything that is going on in and around them. They should listen to each other's problems and try and solve them. Timely analysis of difficulties and problems in a relationship can lead to less unhappiness and anger in the times to come. Communicate with each other openly and logically and strive to find a sensible and logical solution to your problems. Communication is an essential ingredient of a happy and successful married life. Also sharing each other's dreams and desires makes the bond of marriage even stronger. Take each other's opinion and heed to the advice that you receive. Try to analyse situations at home or office in an open and logical manner. Do not give much time and importance to trivial matters and encourage each other to do the same. Try not to say or suggest things that upset your partner. Never convert a discussion into an argument. If for some reason one partner is angry then the other should remain calm and peaceful. Be patient and wait for your partner to cool down, before you can initiate a discussion. Never attack each other personally, that is, avoid insulting each other by attacking each other with complaints, or crying out each other's weaknesses. Also never insult each other in public. Such things cause distress and oppressiveness and merely add bitterness in the relationship.

They increase problems in the married life and may lead to a broken marriage.

Resolve all your problems through mutual discussions. Do not allow anyone else to interfere in your life. This marriage is yours and you have all the right to guard it. Never ever stop talking to each other. No matter what happens, communication has to continue. The strategy should be: even if we are unable to change our circumstances, we will continue to improve them with our love and positive approach.

If your spouse is not talking to you then it should be you who should take the initiative of saying things like, "I love you", or "I am sorry". Hold each other's hands, put an arm around your partner, give each other a head or foot massage. Departing a little from the usual can bring freshness and breathe new life into your relationship. Focus on the good qualities of each other and appreciate them. At the same time, work on your weaknesses and improve upon them. This will make your spouse respect and love you for who you are.

From time to time both the partners need to express their love for each other. Such togetherness brings sweetness and intimacy in the relationship and ends conflicts. Give each other a hug at the end of the day. Hold hands whenever possible. We all like surprises. At times plan things to surprise your partner. Buy each other gifts or plan a short holiday. Such surprises needn't be expensive; what matters is the love that it holds.

Physical intimacy is also very important in a happy married life. Both partners require it equally and both should also respect each other's desires. It is healthy to share your requirements and desires with your spouse. Instead of blaming each other regarding intimacy issues, it is important that both talk to each other and try to resolve their problems. If they are unable to find a solution to their problems, then they should consult a specialist to help them in this regard. Loss of physical intimacy may lead to extramarital affairs, which is not at all a happy situation in a marriage. All possible steps should be taken to remain loyal to your partner. Whenever you feel you are straying away from your marriage, ask yourself this: would I be happy if my partner did this to me? Stabilise and strengthen your marriage with love and understanding for each other. No matter how old your marriage, it should reflect of romanticism and love at all times. It is the love and trust that you share that will take you forward in the years to come and keep you both satisfied and happy forever.

Divorce

Sometimes trivial disagreements lead to full-blown arguments and family discord. It may also sometimes lead to a divorce. At most times neither of the partners realise that is these small wordy encounters between them that have lead to misunderstandings and finally to divorce.

At such a time divorce may seem the only answer to all the problems in the relationship, but life is not pleasant when lived all alone. It is better to focus on the positive qualities of your partner during the marriage, rather then thinking about them after divorce. By then there is no alternative and all that one is left with is regret. If you are ready to compromise and adjust in your second marriage, why not do the same during the first marriage. After all another word for marriage is compromise, whether we agree or not. Also, there is no guarantee that the second marriage will last and be successful. Of course, the past experiences of the first marriage do help you to behave in a more mature and tolerable way the second time around, but what stops you from making those same changes in your current marriage. It is never too late to take a U-turn.

Make your marriage work with all possible efforts. Do away with ego. There is no place for ego in a marriage. Avoid unnecessary arguments, and never bicker in front of your children. Treat each other with resect; your children will also respect you. Your children too need to be treated with respect if you want them to treat you with respect. A husband and wife should generate healthy fun and laughter between themselves and among their family members. Whenever possible, strive to have a happy and joyful atmosphere at home. Laugh and make other laughs. If you are able to achieve this, your marriage will never end in a divorce.

It is not a secret that children of divorced parents are the ones who are affected the most when parents go through a divorce. The entire phase of separation leaves a negative impression on their young minds, and at times such children become rebellious, aggressive, sensitive, irritable, and at times may grow up lacking courage and confidence. They feel shameful and sometimes do not have much faith or trust in themselves or in their relationships. In conclusion, instead of ending your marriage consider eliminating the cause that has ruined your marriage. Disputes are momentary; do not allow them to become the stamp of your divorce. Marriage is a beautiful bond; make all possible efforts to maintain its beauty and fragrance.

One which suits your eyes is beautiful. One which suits your heart is romance.

Generation Gap

The reason behind the difference of thoughts between the new generation and the old generation, that is, between the youngsters of today and the elders of yesterday, is that elders do not like the idea of youngsters defying their orders, and youngsters are not comfortable being rebuked at every action of theirs. The result of such behaviour between the two is a full-blown confrontation.

Having your own views and ideas about things is not bad, but this difference becomes a cause of argument when both sides refuse to understand each others' stand. The elders stick to their age-old views and the youngsters refuse to budge from their ultramodern thinking. What is needed is a compromise and each party should try to meet the other midway. So instead of the young members saying that it is the fault of the elders of the house, and the old people imposing their views on youngsters, both should try to adapt and understand each others situation. No one side can be blamed because both sides are correct in their own unique ways. This age-old battle between both the sides will never be completely over, but an attempt to reduce the arguments can surely be made. This can happen the sooner the elders realise that once they too were young and carefree, and the youngsters realise that they too shall one day become old. If the young generation continues to complain about the older generation, they will never be able to benefit from the experiences of the elders. Similarly, if the older generation accepts and compromises a bit, they will live happier lives in their old age and receive love, respect, and attention from the youngsters. Age-old traditions, and rules and regulations are constantly changing with time; that is why there is a regular change in the attitude of the society.

With changing times the likings of the new generation too have changed.

For instance, the parents want to decorate a wall with a calendar, but the children want to decorate it with some painting. The elders want to put up a picture of God; however, the youngsters want to keep the wall empty. The youngsters want to dispose of the old things of the house while the elders want to hold on to them. Such conflicts happen on a daily basis in most homes. The best remedy for avoiding this is that the elders not interfere in how their children run their homes, and the children on the other hand create some space for the elders in which they can live the way they want to. Majority of the elders in families are unable to adapt themselves to the changing times, and this is what results in confrontations, which then lead to mental tension. Old people should if possible change their ideologies and behaviour according to the changing times. On the other hand, it is also the duty of youngsters to respect and understand the feelings and opinions of the elderly instead of turning a deaf ear to what they are trying to say. Sometimes it is the elderly who come with unique solutions to everyday problems, so respect them instead of humiliating them.

A stressful situation between both sides develops when the elderly criticise more than they can guide.

But, in families where the elderly are respected and loved there are fewer chances of them becoming irritated and angry on trivial matters.

What is important is that there is communication between the children and their parents. Communication should be from both sides. Parents should listen to their children and accept that times have changed, while children should try to use their parents' experiences to live happier and better lives today by not making the mistakes their parents made as youngsters. Though, it is not important that children follow exactly everything that the elders say.

Times have changed and children do not accept blindly whatever the elders say. The elders too on their side should try and receive respect from their children by making suggestions that fit with today's times. The best way is to put yourself in your children's shoes and accordingly suggest.

Instead of being a guardian, try to be your children's friend and guide them in a positive way. If they refuse to listen to you, try and understand the reason behind their refusal. If the denial is not harming their work or hurting anyone, it is okay to let go. Always try to imagine yourself in a similar situation and accordingly analyse the circumstances.

If possible involve your children in the decision-making process. Consult them while planning rules for the household menu, playing, studying, etc. Decide what punishment they get should they make a mistake or break discipline; plan holidays and the daily schedule with them. Decide their amount of study time, how much time should they get to watch TV, how much should they spend surfing the net etc.

When the elders are given proper space in the family and are involved in the major decisions of the family, then they too are able to understand the position and role of the youngsters and share their experiences with them. Such an association brings peace and love in the family and it is a heaven-like environment to live in.

To develop children's talents fully, make them perfect in every work, to take care of merits and demerits and to have knowledge of right and wrong; guardians have to take care of them at every step.

Old Age – Curse or Boon

Old age is natural and a necessary stage of life. There is no real relationship between your present age and old age. There have been many great men and women who made emulated history even after the age of seventy. Some people look old even in their youth while some middle aged and aged people remain active and engaged as if they were still in their youth.

Illness does not come according to age. It depends on the level of your lifestyle and eating habits. Physical, mental, and hormonal changes take place during old age. There is more destruction of cells and tissues of the body than there is growth.

At this stage the majority of sense organs become weak. One gets surrounded by different types of diseases. Due to weakness it becomes difficult to accomplish regular and occasional works. According to doctors and scientists if the rejuvenation of cells in the body is proper, then the sufferings of old age can be avoided.

A person doesn't get really old as long as there is sweetness and enthusiasm in his life. As long as there is ambition in his heart, till then the will power to carry on persists in him. Old age is a state of mind. When a person starts thinking that he is old it is only then that he gets old.

Those who want to live life in the truest sense never think of becoming old. They fight old age and decide to age gracefully. It is only when one gets adamant to not get old that he remains young and stays active and capable till the end. In fact, a person is as much old or young as much as he feels it. A person young at heart does not get old as fast as others.

Generally after spending sixty years or so of our lives we leave our jobs, professions, or regular business life or wind them up to search for and reach a new direction in life. Such a kind of leaving is called retirement.

But retirement from active professional life does not mean you have to actually retire from work. If possible, stay involved with some work or the other even after retirement. An idle person gets old faster. Diseases and depression strike such a person and he begins to ail and wither away. We should treat old age as a useful time to do such things that we were unable to do during our young and busy lives. Let this time of old age be a time of leisure and relaxation. Many people fulfil their hobbies after retirement. For example, some people dedicate their time to gardening, while some people like to spend their maximum time with their family, trying to compensate for the time they did not have when they were working in their younger days. Then there are some aged people who involve themselves in a job depending on their professional experience; some also start their own business after retirement. Not only do they keep themselves busy, but also manage to find a source of income in their old age.

According to psychologists, anything that is done with interest helps a person remain enthusiastic and zealous in life. So is the case in old age. Such people if they keep themselves busy by being involved in activities of their interest protect their health through their enthusiasm and zeal. Learning is very important in any work that is undertaken. In old age, the body may not do be able to strenuous physical work but it is easy and faster for an aged person to learn because of the vast experience that he has with him.

Today there are thousands of retired people who are financially secure and physically fit too. Such people can become a major source of reform in the society. They can contribute their services to educational institutions, social organisations, or to resident welfare associations. Inactivity and idleness is the main cause of depression in old age.

Keep away old age

It is certain that old age will come but maintaining a proper life style and following a good health regime can prolong it further. As long as the cells of the body get rejuvenated regularly, our body will stay fit and we will manage to delay old age. When there is an obstruction in this continuous cell growth process and the growth of the body cells slows down, then the body starts getting old.

We can slow down the process of ageing by following a proper diet that is nutritious and healthy.

In old age reduce your diet to almost half of what you were consuming in your younger days; but don't be a miser in drinking water. Low consumption of water can lead to various illnesses.

Natural foods like sprouted cereals, seeds, dry fruits (soaked), seasonal fruits, green vegetables and salads (carrot, beetroot, vegetable marrow, tomato, cucumber, etc.) should be taken in their natural form. *Amla* (Indian gooseberry) and honey are the most important and should be consumed regularly.

Drink a glass of vegetable juice daily (cucumber, bottle gourd, tomato, white pumpkin, spinach, *bathua* leaves (white goose poot), corriander leaves, mint, etc.).

The daily consumption of the juice of 50 gm amla, 75 gm beetroot, 250 gm carrot, 25 gm raw turmeric, 5 gm ginger helps keeps old age away.

Refined flour, tea, coffee, salt, sugar, spices, fats, fried foods, non-vegetarian items, etc., should be avoided as far as possible. Avoid smoking and the intake of alcohol.

Realised usage: Take four teaspoons of wheat and one teaspoon of fenugreek seeds; wash them properly and soak them for 24 hours in half a glass of water. After 24 hours filter it and add to it the juice of half a lemon, 2 gm of dry ginger powder, and two teaspoons of honey. Drink this on an empty stomach every day. This drink is very nutritive and acts as a digestive and an energiser. If possible, consume sprouted wheat and fenugreek also.

Freedom from diseases: To keep yourself free from diseases adopt naturopathy or natural therapy.

Make old age better

If you are ready to experiment with new things in life and want to live a life full of zest and youth make sure you try the following:

- Walking is a good source of exercise; make it your everyday habit
- Laughing is not only a good exercise and a treatment procedure but it is also a useful means to keep yourself tension free. Laugh aloud wholeheartedly
- Adopt positive thinking; this will help maintain happiness and enthusiasm
- Avoid negative thinking and be happy
- Try to bring about an improvement in your desires and aspirations according to the situation
- Be self-confident and keep your morale high in difficult situations
- Try to experience every incident of life in a light and joyful manner; do not take life too seriously
- To remain mentally fit, encourage your mind to do mental exercises – solve puzzles and maths problems, figure out riddles, decipher old writings and pictures, crack codes, etc.; these keep your mind alert and busy
- Try to learn and master something new; this increases the creativity of a person and a person doesn't get old early
- Study literature that interests you and which brings about a feeling of modernity within you
- Maintain a diary and write in it regularly; analyse yourself and the situations and people around you

- Adopt some physical work as a part of your daily routine; it could be an interest in gardening, drawing, painting, sculpting, etc.
- Inhaling deep breaths induces deep sleep
- Try not to disagree about everything; learn to agree as well
- Music is a good medium that can be used to keep away tiredness and sadness in old age.

Some other ways to slow down the process of ageing are as follows:

To avoid wrinkles on the face tighten your lips and then spread a smile as broad as possible. Keep your face in this position till a count of six. Then extend your lips in a manner of whistling. Keep them in this position till a count of ten.

To avoid the problem of hanging cheeks, fill air in your mouth and shut it. Cheeks should be lifted upwards. Now place your fists on your blown cheeks and try to press your cheeks with your fists. With the air pressure in your mouth, try to stop the air from escaping when you press with your fists. Then slowly release the air from the mouth. Repeat this ten times a day.

Wrinkles develop on the skin due to ageing. To avoid them, use oil to massage your face and body. Oil massage gives life force to the body in old age. Massaging helps the muscles of the skin to become flexible and prevents wrinkles from developing.

With your left thumb, press the area between your right wrist and elbow, for two minutes every day. This increases life force and youth is retained for a longer period. Ageing is delayed and you appear younger.

Style of living

Old age is seen as a big problem in the world. Some of us even treat aged people in the family as a burden. Sometimes the aged people themselves begin to consider themselves as a burden on their children. They stay unhappy and dissatisfied. Most aged people complain that they are in a miserable situation.

In old age make children realise about their right and wrong as a friend not as a critic. Don't blame their working style rather tell them how to do it in a much better and easier way. Give full responsibility of the house and business to the children, but keep some wealth safely for your own needs. Restrict your needs according to the circumstances.

After transferring all your responsibilities to your children, let them work voluntarily. Keep watch on their work and make them capable in every respect.

You have lived your life in your own way. Now let your children live it their way.

To live together happily and peacefully, it is important to tolerate the weaknesses of each other and appreciate the greatness of each other. You should keep in mind that everyone has good qualities as well as weaknesses. It is also not true that you may be right every time and the others wrong. That is why others' opinions and feelings should be respected.

Words of a satisfied aged person

I am carefree. I have given my family all the responsibilities. I do whatever my children say, I eat whatever they serve, and I laugh and play with my grandchildren. If my children make some mistake I keep silent. I don't create obstacles in their way or work. Whenever they seek advice or consult me, I try to explain through my experiences. I don't care how much they honour my suggestions. I am not persistent that they follow my instructions. I am not worried if they again commit a mistake. Of course, if again they come to me for advice, I don't get angry; instead I again give them advice.

Loneliness

Loneliness definitely is a curse for old age. Old couples when they lose their partner become lonely. The memories of the past hurt them and the feeling of loneliness disturbs them. This situation can be overcome by a strong will power and intelligence.

At the age when parents need the children the most, at most times the children are not able to give that support. This is a natural and normal procedure. Children being busy with their work and responsibilities are unable to devote all the time to their parents. They also get busy with their own families and children, in the process making their parents lonely and bored. But this is a cycle that has continued for ages and that is why it is important for the aged to accept this situation gracefully. Instead they should engage themselves in some creative activities or in activities that they enjoy. If possible, they should find way by which they can help others.

Results of mental status

Many aged people develop mental illnesses in old age. This could be due to the loss of their life partner, retirement, financial crisis, social problems, or insult or negligence by their family. Such situations can have a disastrous effect on their minds and they may suffer from mental ailments.

Therefore, whenever possible the aged should look out for positive and joyful means to keep themselves busy and happy.

Preparation of old age in the years of youth

Old age is the biggest truth of life. Nobody can escape old age. One day we will all become old, but old age usually consists of illnesses and helplessness. But it is not necessary that this be true in all cases. It is up to each individual to have a happy adulthood. If we want to be fit in old age then it is very important that we take care of our health while we are young.

It is perceived that walking is the most important exercise, especially for aged people. People who walk daily to keep their body fit are able to prevent stiffness in their legs and hands. Aged people should do light exercises, if possible. Whenever possible, aged people should keep themselves involved in some activity or the other; being busy will help them remain mentally fit. Special care should be taken of the diet of old people; they should avoid food with excess salt, sugar and oil. Also, they should avoid fried foods and consume more of fruits and vegetables. If possible, they should try and reduce their weight to normal. By this they will remain active and energetic.

For a healthy old age, one should start taking care from the age of forty. Avoid smoking and reduce alcohol intake.

Take special care of your eyes and ears when you are young; old age is associated with the loss of hearing and vision. Also take good care of your teeth while you can; by the time you become old, the teeth would begin to decay and eating then becomes a hurdle. To be able to eat properly through your old age, it is very important that care be taken while you are young.

According to your capacity and requirement, keep some money exclusively for yourself during old age. This well-protected money should be totally under your control. Instead of distributing the rights of ownership to the children, the elders should have a will made. This way the assets remain with them throughout their lives. Though this may sound selfish and degrading, but it is true that elders who possess property and a good source of income even in their old age are respected and looked after by their children better than those aged people who distribute their possessions to their children. Becoming financially dependent in old age is almost equal to living in hell.

Support of reverse mortgage for senior citizens

Reverse mortgage was started in 2007 in India. It is very popular in foreign countries.

Reverse mortgage comes in handy for those senior citizens who only have their own house to live in but don't have any source of income and don't have any support from their children. This scheme is entirely different from the general mortgage system. By taking a loan under general mortgage a person has to pay back monthly. But in accordance to reverse mortgage, senior citizens can get a monthly income throughout their life by mortgaging their house to the bank. This also allows them to live in the same house throughout their lives. In this scheme the bank evaluates the cost of the house and ascertains a monthly income of the person who has selected this scheme according to factors such as life span of the borrower and the spouse.

The bank evaluates the cost of the house from time to time. It increases the monthly income as the market rate of the house increases in an appropriate ratio.

In the case of the death of the husband or wife, the other partner can continue to live in the house that is under reverse mortgage. If in the duration of the agreement both the husband and wife die then the bank sells the house to cover their portion of money and the rest is distributed between the aged couples dependents or given to their legal heir as mentioned in the will.

However, there is a provision that the bank will first give a chance to the legal heirs of the person to buy the house.

Income received through reverse mortgage scheme is tax free because the government understands that this money is only a loan and not an income. Thus, now any Indian senior citizen who possesses his own house cannot consider himself helpless.

For safety of old age

All aged people should hold a cover for mediclaim, accidental insurance, and life insurance.

To maintain a regular income in old age, make some investments or invest in some pension plans.

It doesn't matter at what age you retire, but it does matter what you possess at the time of retirement.

Old age becomes a blessing (boon) if one is physically fit, has a regular source of income, possesses ownership rights of property, and has been able to get all the children settled and married. Now he can enjoy the rest of his life with peace and happiness.

Occasionally retired persons think of old age as inconvenient and force themselves into trouble, but the truth is just the opposite of it. If plans are made for the future and retirement then life will not become a burden; instead it would become a symbol of immense peace and happiness.

Stress Management

Stress is a problem that we face every day. Stress dominates us while eating, walking, working, and even when we are sitting all alone. A little bit of stress is not a problem but it becomes a problem when it increases to uncontrollable limits and begins to affect the everyday functioning of people.

Symptoms of mental stress

1. Sleeplessness, nightmares, etc
2. Irritability and anger
3. Headache or heaviness in the head
4. Any kind of intoxication
5. Constantly talking about one's own problems
6. Unable to concentrate in any subject or work
7. Wasting time and postponing work
8. Chewing nails
9. Negative thinking
10. Erratic thoughts
11. Being boastful
12. Getting perturbed again and again
13. Illusion of undesired happenings
14. Having a weak memory
15. Driving carelessly
16. Disinterest in social, family, and business matters
17. Constant feeling of insecurity
18. Shaking of knees while sitting

19. Repeated intake of stimulating drinks such as tea, coffee, etc.
20. Blinking too often
21. Hesitant nature or fickle minded
22. Shouting while saying anything, banging doors, and losing temper
23. Inability to take any decision
24. Constant feeling of lethargy

Effects of stress

When the mind is not peaceful, then how can the body be healthy? Ever notice how we stay tense for things out of which 90 percent don't even occur? Common diseases due to stress are:

1. Hypertension (high blood pressure)
2. Heart diseases
3. Asthma
4. Migraine
5. Spondylosis
6. Acidity, peptic ulcer
7. Menstrual irregularity
8. Insomnia (sleeplessness)
9. Diabetes
10. Backache
11. Shoulder pain
12. Stable tiredness
13. Depression
14. Mental weakness
15. Weak eyesight
16. Paucity of semen
17. Early ageing

18. Constipation
19. Cough and cold
20. Lose or gain weight
21. Disturbed mind (behaving violently with others, abusing and rebuking servants, misbehaving with spouse, rebuking and arguing with colleagues in the office)

It is astonishing that all those who are mentally dull by birth, generally don't have any physical diseases. This example indicates that those who are free from mental tension are also free from most of the mental diseases.

Reasons for mental stress

1. Ailing and unhealthy body
2. Comparative point of view and competition; bitterness and feeling of jealousy
3. Negative attitude
4. Excessive workload
5. Fear of failure
6. Unemployment and other financial problems
7. Unfulfilment of desires
8. Extremely ambitious nature
9. Any kind of intoxication or addiction
10. Insecure atmosphere and uncooperative colleagues
11. Getting influenced by others very easily
12. Involved in illegal work or occupation
13. Being excessively sentimental (taking everything to heart)
14. Harsh-natured partner or spouse
15. Noisy and loud atmosphere at workplace
16. Incapable subordinates

17. Failure in physical relations or love affairs
18. Bearing the brunt of insults, taunts, and displeasure
19. Regularly telling lies
20. Ill effects of television on subconscious mind
21. Feeling of dissatisfaction
22. Death of someone dear
23. Termination from service or incurring losses in business
24. Non-completion of desired work
25. Ill treatment by others
26. Having a materialistic lifestyle
27. Dominating financial point of view on life
28. Lack of time and suffering from laziness
29. Not able to choose priorities in life
30. Lack of an organised lifestyle
31. Lack of self-confidence
32. Lack of faith in God
33. Prominence of vicious and royal lifestyle
34. Imbalance and disparity between the heart and mind
35. Not believing in work and only depending on destiny; having blind faith or superstitions.

Freedom from tension

1. The most easiest way to get freedom from tension is by choosing to have a positive attitude
2. Regular morning walks exercises, *shatkarma, yogasana, pranayama,* meditation, *shavasana,* and *yognidra* are some very effective ways to release stress
3. Keep the "remote control" of happiness in your own hands; do not allow it to go to others. If you get stressed by what others say to you or about you, then it means

that the remote control of your happiness is in others' hands.

4. Sometimes some problems are followed by great opportunities. Try to find the root cause of your problems and find their solutions because problems come with their solutions.
5. Do not waste time trying to find out who is wrong or right; rather think about what is wrong or right.
6. Look for positive qualities in those with whom you have problems; you won't be disappointed.
7. Try to understand others points of view, because you can change yourself but not others.
8. Finish necessary tasks before they become urgent. Learn to divide and choose your work.
9. Utilise time properly.
10. Learn to say "No".
11. Choose competent workers.
12. If you have to do many tasks all at once, do not panic; prioritise your work and soon you would have completed each task successfully.
13. Remember, there is always scope for progress in all situations.
14. If someone tells you about your faults, welcome him because this is in your favour.
15. Identify the fear attached with any difficulty and find the ways to overcome this fear.
16. Truth never dies; if you are on the path of truth then there is no need to worry under any circumstances.
17. Detachment does not cause tension.
18. Compromise with situations. If you can't change them then don't get sad thinking about it. Just move on. Remember, time is one of the best healers.

19. Improve yourself and the world will improve on its own.
20. If you try to bring happiness and peace in others' life then you yourself will experience mental happiness and peace.
21. When a worry bothers, stop thinking on that topic and concentrate on some other topic because thinking on one topic for too long increases tension.
22. If someone behaves in an immoral manner then neglect him rather than hating him or holding a grudge against him.
23. Learn to be forgivable and tolerable, and always keep smiling.
24. Be childish with children and enjoy your time playing with them
25. Retain or develop some new hobbies that delight you – reading of good books, listening to music, learning how to play a musical instrument.
26. Make sure you get complete sleep.
27. To rock on a rocking chair gives the feeling of lightness and mental pleasure.
28. Whosoever takes birth, it is certain that he will also die. Relatives meet in one family and then get separated. Then why to grieve and sorrow?
29. In case you feel like weeping, then it is beneficial to burst into tears and cry yourself out. This will make you feel lighthearted.
30. Utilise and enjoy whatever you have rather than being sad and worried that one day you may not have the same
31. Don't feel sad for mistakes made in the past, rather think about the future. Concentrate fully to make the present successful. If you do creative work today, then

the past mistakes will diminish and the future will certainly benefit.

32. Is your office or house filled with useless things? If so it will create useless tension and nothing else. At home and in office, clean and clear your almirah, table, drawer etc., from time-to-time. Throw away useless things such as papers, books, newspapers, magazines, etc.

33. Get financial planning by purchasing the following insurances –

Higher education and marriage of children, hospital expenses, in case of illness or accident, provision of income; in case of accident or disability, provision for retired life, emergency funds. In case of untimely death of the earning member, maintenance of income to the existing family member.

Each day in life is precious. Make each day of your life precious. Don't regret any certain day. If good days bring happiness then bad days give excess of experience. Both of these are very important for life.

The Power of Thought

Your thoughts are generated and influenced by the things that you observe, feel, imagine, and to things that you get attracted to. A person becomes the same as his ideology. Our conduct is influenced by the type of thoughts we live with. The kind of companions we make, type of information we collect, our interests, inspirations, etc., are all because of the power of our thoughts. Our personal space is shaped according to our beliefs and ideas.

Your thoughts are powerful. Never let them sway towards the negative. Always think that whatever we wish to attain can be achieved by us – love, happiness, success, peace, prosperity, professional growth, status in society, and much more.

Wealth and poverty, both are the results of our thinking. It means, we become rich or poor according to the way we can control our thoughts.

We become what we think. If we think we are poor, good for nothing, not capable of doing anything then we will become poor and useless forever.

The way we look at the world, so will the world seem to us.

The law of attraction says that similar things attract similar things. That is why when you think about something, you attract similar thoughts towards you.

Your present thoughts are building your future life. Things that you think about and focus on the most begin to appear in your life. Most times, whatever you think happens; that is why a person should be careful about his thinking.

Never underestimate the power of your thoughts. All good thoughts give birth to good actions in due course of time. Negative thoughts bring negativity with them. Leave the bad and accept the good.

But if you continue to get wrong ideas in your mind that provoke you to do wrong things again and again then consider the end result of your actions rather than the feeling behind that thought to do that particular act. Think, what will be the result if I do this? We all know from our past experiences that wrong actions bring wrong results, and that is why we should stay away from negative actions. If you do not get along with someone, instead of focusing on the negative aspects of that person, try to focus on the positive and with time you will both begin to get along.

A person's ideology is influenced by the company he keeps and the stuff that he reads or sees around him. A person is judged by the ideas he endorses. Thoughts have the power to shape your life and future. Observe and analyse thoughts that rise every moment in your mind. Retain positive thoughts and discard negative ones.

Success is not attained by the size of the brain. It is attained by the size of the thoughts. Thus, think big and positive. You should always have the courage to think big. Dreams should be such that can be achieved in reality; be prepared to work with full devotion and concentration for something special. Then see if your thoughts have the strength to properly utilise your internal powers, resources, and expectations. You will be surprised how you yourself are not aware of the presence of such things in you.

Mind Power

The mind is the strongest power in the possession of human beings. By virtue of mind power, man is able to convert the impossible to the possible. He is able to overcome his biggest problems in life and sometimes succeeds in doing tasks that are almost undoable. There are two types of mind: (1) conscious mind (2) sub-conscious mind.

The conscious mind remains active only when we are awake and has only 10% of the powers. The sub-conscious mind is active for 24 hours and has 90% of the powers. The conscious mind is in the brain but the sub-conscious mind is behind the navel, which is also called the solar plexus. The sub-conscious mind is connected to the conscious mind through the vagus nerve.

Work and powers of the conscious mind

The conscious mind can work only in the physical world and within the physical body.

1. It controls all five organs of action (hands, legs, vocal cord, excretory organs, and the reproductive organs.
2. It controls the information of all the five sense organs (eyes, ears, nose, tongue, and skin).
3. It controls the thoughts.
4. The power of logic resides within the conscious mind.
5. The analytic power also resides within the conscious mind.
6. The act of interpretation too is done through the conscious mind.

7. The conscious mind is responsible for the intelligence quotient of a person.
8. The conscious mind has to be alert enough to recognise and grab opportunities.
9. The judging power too is within the conscious mind.
10. The conscious mind aids in decision making and also helps in its implementation.
11. The conscious mind develops different kinds of desires.
12. The power of liking too resides with the conscious mind but when there is difficulty in deciding about the likings then the sub-conscious mind steps in.
13. No message reaches the sub-conscious mind without the desire of the conscious mind. The conscious mind works like a watchman at all times.

Work and powers of the sub-conscious mind

The sub-conscious mind can travel in this subtle world in unlimited forms.

1. Reflex actions, that is, automatic actions, such as to shudder on hearing a loud noise, to pull back your hand when it touches a hot thing, etc., are done by the sub-conscious mind.
2. The conscience is the warning of the sub-conscious mind to the conscious mind to not do anything wrong or undesired.
3. Telepathy means our immense will power attracts our most desired person towards us and the person, who may be living miles away, gets the same thoughts as we are getting. This is the power of the sub-conscious mind.
4. The memory power is the power of the sub-conscious mind and this power is unimaginable.

5. Emotions are of two kinds: positive and negative. These emotions or the emotional quotient are controlled by the subconscious mind.
6. The subconscious mind is a treasure trove of knowledge of which most of us are unaware.
7. The power to take a decision at times of difficulty lies with the sub-conscious mind.
8. Creation of opportunity: Whatever you want to become or want to acquire can be done through the sub-conscious mind.
9. Creative thinking: Powers of creative thinking also lie with the sub-conscious mind.
10. Magnetic Power: Any desired thing or person can be attracted by the sub-conscious mind.
11. Solution of problems: Whenever you face problems in again the sub-conscious mind is ready to help you out.
12. Healing: In cases where medicines fail to provide any treatment or improvement, the power of the sub-conscious mind aids in the healing process.
13. Spiritual Quotient: Maintaining congruency between thinking, speaking, and doing is also a power of the sub-conscious mind.
14. Personal God: Our inner sub-conscious mind is our own personal God, who supports us and provides consolation and guidance to us at times of difficulty and confusion. It gives us the power to carry out our tasks and also creates positive circumstances to achieve our goals. It also gives happiness, peace, and good health. When we decide to do any great work then it helps us by providing us the cosmic power.

The sub-conscious mind possesses unlimited knowledge and power.

Specialities of the mind

The conscious mind possesses the thinking powers, the will power, and the power of logic, whereas the unconscious mind has no such powers; it merely works as a faithful servant without any evidence or argument.

The conscious mind possesses the power of discretion. If for instance, all the thoughts are sent to the sub-conscious mind without using the conscious mind then the sub-conscious mind starts obeying the orders of both the good and the bad thoughts that arise in the mind. This can pose several difficulties in life.

The sub-conscious mind quickly obeys the orders of negative thoughts; hence, by using one's discretionary powers negative thoughts can be prevented to reach the sub-conscious mind and instead positive thoughts can be adopted.

Positive Thoughts	Negative Thoughts
My future is bright	My future is bleak
All people are reliable	No one is reliable
My life is without problems	My life is full of problems
People love me very much	No one loves me
I am capable of doing many things	I am capable of doing nothing
The present times are favourable for me	The present times are unfavourable for me
It is very easy to earn money	It is not easy to earn money
I love my profession	My profession is useless
I can do this work	I can't do this work
I have plenty to give	I have nothing to give
I have enough time and sources at my disposal	I do not have enough time and sources at my disposal

Don't use negative language, and if someone uses it, don't let it reach your sub-conscious mind. For instance, if someone says the following: You don't have sense. You can't understand.

You won't be able to do anything in your life. You will never improve yourself.

One day you will defame the honour of our family.

My fortune was destroyed as I had to manage with you.

Our perceptions become the same as our thoughts and reach the sub-conscious mind.

Positive Emotions	**Negative Emotions**
Mercy	Fear
Love	Jealousy
Forgiveness	Anger
Compassion	Hatred
Gratitude	Worry
Faith	Sadism
Tolerance	Intolerance
Hope	Hopeless
Nobleness	Self-interest

Four stages of the mind

Electromagnetic waves are produced in the brain. These waves fulfil the power required by the brain to work regularly. These waves are directly related to the activeness of our brain. The more actively the brain works, the more is the frequency of the waves and as the frequency of the waves increases the requirement of oxygen too increases.

BETA: 14–35 waves per second – conscious stage.

ALPHA: 7–14 waves per second – sub-conscious stage.

THETA: 4–7 waves per second – sleeping stage.

DELTA: 1–4 waves per second – unconscious stage.

Utility method of powers of the sub-conscious mind

In the Alfa stage, whatever information we give to our sub-conscious mind gets stored and later they appear in reality in the outer world.

We can go in to alpha stage in two ways:

First, by the natural way, that is, ten minutes before going to sleep or ten minutes after getting up from sleep.

Second, is relaxation according to our desire. Relaxation means:

1. To sit calmly in a peaceful place
2. Slowly inhale and exhale by deep breathing
3. Relax every part of body one by one with every breath
4. To feel yourself relaxed and separated from the body
5. Start reverse counting from 20 to 1. Start saying to yourself with every count that I am going deep and deep in to mental relaxation. I am in a fully peaceful situation – now there is no thought, no desire. My sub-conscious mind is ready to accept all suggestions and resolutions.

When you are in the Alfa stage, you are very near the sub-conscious mind even though you are fully conscious. At this stage whatever imagination or assumption or objective you think of will be marked on your sub-conscious mind and will unknowingly easily transform you to achieve that objective. The sub-conscious mind is a treasure of our maximum powers and skills. If we can utilise it fully we can shape our life according to our wish.

Visualisation

We can also call visualisation as the programming of the sub-conscious mind.

Imagine one of your objectives as if you have actually achieved it and you are living with it in reality; think that it actually happened. In such a situation whatever you think or imagine will be marked on your sub-conscious mind and unknowingly the sub-conscious mind will regularly influence the waves of your conscious mind and the body and you will be surprised to see that you have proceed towards that objective and also achieved it.

(Exercise this for at least 21 days for short-term targets. For long-term targets exercise it for 3 months to 1 year, till you have mastered and achieved it.)

Catalyst for programming of the sub-conscious mind

(1) Fasting, (2) silence, (3) positive thoughts, (4) prayer, (5) meditation.

Method of sending messages to the conscious mind through the unconscious mind

The sub-conscious mind sends messages to the conscious mind by different methods, but the conscious mind should be inactive at that time.

1. Flashes: Sometimes we are unable to get the answer to some of our questions, but afterwards when we sit peacefully then all of a sudden we get a thought and also get the answer to those questions.
2. Intuition: This is also called immediate understanding. Every day we live a normal life, but suddenly one day we want to do something new or different; this is called intuition.
3. Impulses: An impulse is when we get a thought again and again regularly and this thought distresses us till we work according to that thought.
4. Dreams: Whenever you dream of something, utilise it rather than considering it true.

Utilisation of the power of mind

Before pregnancy: The husband and wife should mentally have a picture of the kind of child they would like to have to influence how the new born looks like.

During pregnancy: Many things can be taught to the unborn child by programming of the mind.

Developing stage of child: The child can be made a good and valiant citizen by programming him from childhood.

On reaching adulthood: To fulfil your aims and objectives; to leave behind your negative qualities; to develop your positive qualities; to control the ageing process; to get solutions to your problems. Before sleeping think about every aspect of your problem, after that you won't need to think anything. After waking up you will realise that the solution of the problem has automatically developed in your brain. Before sleeping don't carry negative thoughts from watching T.V. or listening to the radio. At that time the sub-conscious mind is active; keep it calm and positive.

Remember

- The weight of the brain is just 2% in comparison to that of the body, but it utilises 20% blood, 20% oxygen, and 20% nutrition in comparison to that of the rest of the body.
- In an average only 2% of the brain's capability is utilised. Even the most greatest of people have utilised only 15% of it. 70% of diseases occur through our mind and our thoughts.

Look beyond your boundaries and explore yourself

- 95% people don't know what they want in life
- 3% people know what they want but they don't know how to achieve it
- 1% people know it and also achieve it but are unable to experience its pleasure because till then they have spoiled their health
- 1% people know it, achieve it and also experience its pleasure

Out of all the inventions till now, the most important invention is the invention of the astonishing power of the mind and the knowledge of its use.

A Positive Attitude

We all want to be successful in life and we make continuous efforts to achieve this success. Of all the positive qualities that we have – education, knowledge, honesty, hard working, action-oriented, efficient, loyal, – a good attitude is the most important one to make us successful in our endeavours.

As is our attitude so will be our thoughts.

As is our thought so we will speak.

As we speak so we will work.

As we work so will be our habits.

As are our habits so will be our character.

As is our character so will be our destiny.

A positive attitude is directly related to health, courage, enthusiasm, success, and habits.

In our lives knowledge and expertise play ten percent of the role and the rest ninety percent of the role is played by our attitude that is hidden and is not visible – our values, principles, standards, ethics, beliefs, etc. When an egg is broken with external force it leads to the end of a life, whereas when an egg breaks from the internal force used by the chick then a new life starts. Similarly, every good thing starts with an internal power and force.

Two people visualise the same thing differently because of their differing attitudes. Just as attitude can help raise a person to great heights, it can also crush him if not used properly and sensibly. An optimist finds a good opportunity in every problem whereas a pessimist finds difficulty in every opportunity.

A person who is eager to work has many ideas to share and do good work, but a person who is not willing to work has many excuses to avoid the work.

A positive attitude inspires us to move further and to not get disheartened even when unfavourable conditions develop.

Negative attitudes that are affected by negativities such as ego, inferiority complex, enmity, friction, selfishness, presumptions, etc., make a person hopeless, desperate, and distressed.

A positive attitude shows us a clear direction and prevents us from the falls in the battle of life.

A negative attitude gives birth to suspicion and leads to downfall.

A positive attitude results in success, self-confidence, happiness, enthusiasm, good health, a balanced life, expansion and growth, betterment of family members, prosperity, and in achievement of higher goals.

A negative attitude results in failure, tension, frustration, anger, hatred, indecisiveness, doubt, suspicion, unfaithfulness, stress, and in ailments such as high blood pressure, ulcers, heart problems, etc.

A person with a positive attitude thanks the past, works in the present, and plans for the future.

A person with a negative attitude blames his past, accuses his present, and cries for his future.

An example of positive attitude

Soldier: Sir, the enemy has surrounded us from all directions.

Major: Very good, now we can attack in any direction.

For your attitude, only you are responsible, no one else.

If you want to be happy with your attitude and have decided that you will remain happy no matter what, then no one can make you unhappy.

Success starts from the mind. If you want to be successful then you have to develop the capability to look beyond barriers, obstructions, and failures.

If you dislike something then change it. If you can't change it, then change your attitude. No matter where you work and what the nature of your work is, the one base of your success is — a positive attitude.

The most important change in a person's life is the change in his attitude; the results of adopting a positive attitude are always excellent.

Pleasure or pain is nothing in itself. It is a kind of mental state. It is a feeling of reaction to an incident in our conscious state. If we feel happy because of something then it becomes the reason of our happiness. If we feel sad because of something then it becomes the reason of our sadness.

Set Your Goal

To live without a goal, or aim, is to waste time, energy, and money. It is only those who set goals who become successful in achieving their goals.

Those who don't have their own goals, work towards the goals of others.

Attitude has a direct relationship with the subconscious mind; when you decide to do something with burning desire then the whole world becomes your partner in helping you fulfil your goal.

So, first develop the burning desire. Then decide on it, and later make a firm commitment to fulfil it. Desire alone cannot do anything (because it can be deferred).

Decision achieves a bit something. But, a goal, or aim, does everything.

So, don't have only desire in life; make it a habit to set and achieve your goal. It is only a firm commitment that helps a person achieve his goal.

When the commitment is strong and firm then it does not matter how long the path is, how difficult the way is, or how many obstacles or problems come in the way. Today, the number of great personalities who we honour and remember with great respect reached those great heights because of the power of their strong commitment. It is a miracle of burning desire and a strong commitment that with an artificial leg Sudha Chandran achieved great heights in the sphere of classical music and films with her dance as well as acting.

Eklavya, was not disheartened when his Guru Dronacharya refused to give him lessons in the field of archery. He adopted Dronacharya's statue as his guru and completed his strong commitment by becoming a better bowman than Arjun.

Vishnu Gupt Kautilya "Chanakya" at last established a world famous government in Magadh and fulfilled his pledge, inspite of suffering insult and defeat several times.

If the goal is big, comparatively the achievement too will be big. The person who fixes big goals, gets success and utilises his time in the best way possible, whereas a person who sets small goals is only able to utilise his time partially to achieve his goals.

Keep your sight fixed on the goal and constantly keep moving towards it without slack.

If the route is beautiful then it is very important to know where it leads to. But if the destination is beautiful then it does not matter how easy or difficult the path is. Just keep moving on it.

Obstacles are visible only when your sight is diverted from the destination.

To attain your goal, work with full concentration and immerse yourself in it.

When obstinacy, or craziness, is attached with some good commitment then it becomes a strong commitment as well as a strong pledge.

Discuss your commitment with your spouse and friends to provide additional strength to your commitment.

If you analyse your commitment from time to time then you will definitely be a winner.

To achieve your goal, once you have committed, enthusiasm has a major role to play; it should be regular and endless.

When we set out to achieve something, we put in all our enthusiasm and power at the onset. After some time when one of the targets gets achieved, we become convinced that nothing can stop us from achieving our goal and becoming successful. Such a feeling tends to make us a bit relaxed and at times weakens our efforts to achieve our goals. Beware of such a situation. No matter what, never let your efforts become sluggish. The goal may look easy and achievable, but a slight lax and you may never be able to achieve your goal.

A goal should be SMART:

S – Specific

M – Measurable

A – Achievable

R – Realistic

T – Time-bound

(1) **Specific**: What needs to be achieved?

For example

What do I want in life?

What do I want to do in life?

What do I want to become in life?

What kind of a life do I want to live?

(2) **Measurable**: Goals should be made such that its development can be measured and comparative analysis can be done. By measuring development towards a goal makes the achievement easy. That makes you realise that how far or close you are from your goal.

(3) **Achievable**: Your goal should be full of challenge but should not be out of reach.

(4) **Realistic**: If your goal is unrealistic it will not be achieved fully. For example, a person desiring to reduce his weight from 100 kilos to 50 kilos in 30 days.

(5) **Time-Bound**: Make your goal achievable within a particular time frame. If you do not fix a time to your goal, you will keep postponing it and it will never be achieved.

Priority

To give priority to a particular work means that work has to be done before any other task. One of the reasons of success in life is, first, setting your priorities and, second, setting them right. Our priorities keep changing according to the situation we are in at a particular time in our lives.

The role of priority is important in every aspect of life. Be it business, society, family, or friendship, priorities have to decided everywhere.

Priorities may be divided into four parts:

1. Important and urgent: Such as in an emergency (illness, accident, etc.).
   Immediately disposing problems.
   For completion of certain work in a stipulated time – project schemes, meetings, preparations, etc.
2. Important and non-urgent: Such as rescue operations, building relationships, recognising opportunities, planning, necessary rest, to authorise.
3. Non-important and urgent: Such as obstacles, useless phone calls, mail and post, some reports and some meetings.
4. Non-Important and non-urgent: Such as idle chatter, work done to only look busy, attending some useless and lengthy phone calls, time wasters, non-important post, excess watching of television, oversleeping.

Make it a point to complete important tasks before they become urgent. Don't leave important tasks so that non-important tasks can be completed.

Success

Success cannot be granted it has to be acquired. Targets and goals do not appear near until we strive to reach them. If one way to success is lost or hidden, then another has to be found or create. Statues do not make themselves; they are carved out of the huge stone and painstakingly sculpted.

Each one of us has extraordinary powers. It is up to us to make strong commitments, keep intact our self-confidence, work with dedication, and work hard against all odds to achieve our goals. We all want to be successful. We all work hard and try to achieve and acquire our goals. But, not all of us become successful. The one who becomes successful is the one who does things differently. So, along with working hard it is also important to work smart.

The first step towards success is the feeling of being successful.

Always try to attain excellence in your work. Do it so well that no one else can do it any better. By achieving excellence in such a way success is achieved and this gradually becomes a process of regular betterment.

For becoming successful, it is important to be happy with what you have. Never feel bad because of what you do not have. Whatever work you start doing, make it a habit to do it with full concentration and energy. A work started halfheartedly is always left incomplete.

A clever person tries to benefit from his own experiences but a successful person tries to benefit from others' experiences.

Steps of Success

1. See dreams and dream big; imagine how your future life will be if you can live it like you want to live in your dreams
2. Set your goals: Be committed to whatever you want and keep your efforts according to your goals.
3. Make plans: Collect all the relative resources for the work that you will do and then prioritise your activities accordingly
4. Adopt a positive attitude: A person who is positive and thinks positive too is able to achieve the maximum heights of success
5. Be enthusiastic: It is only when you have self-belief and enthusiasm only then are you able to know the secret of success
6. Be courageous: To achieve your goal continue on the path with courage, no matter what.
7. Understand the importance of team work: The more the people you take along with you, the more your strength will increase and the faster you will achieve success.
8. Capability of leadership: Move forward recognising your talents and capabilities and take full responsibility for the extra work that you put in. The capabilities of leadership develop further when you go a step forward and take responsibilities.
9. Sharpen edges: As the sharp edges of an axe are required to cut wood, in the same way develop your mind, power, and spirituality by yoga, meditation, games, health and management knowledge so that success becomes yours.
10. Always be ready to learn new things: Try to learn something new and special every day; don't go to sleep

till you have learnt something new. This information can be gained from books, internet, T.V., or by talking to people. New thoughts are developed in the mind by the new information gained on a daily basis.

11. Complete work within the time limit: Many people among us are afraid of time limits, but the truth is that until a time limit is set for a particular work, the work does not complete in an efficient and desirable manner. People who complete the tasks allotted to them within the time limit set are able to acquire additional work from their clients. Also, at times of emergency this proves to be beneficial.

12. Communicate with colleagues: Use your capability of communication. To be successful, maintaining mutual communication is also important. Try and maintain a positive relationship with your colleagues, seniors, and juniors at your workplace. If possible, try to become popular among your colleagues. Don't hesitate to help them. Learn to share your thoughts with others. This will encourage your colleagues to talk about their problems with you. Gain expertise in both the art of writing and talking. Whenever possible send daily reports of your work to your boss. By maintaining such a connection he will be able to know about your work.

13. Try to compete with yourself: Whenever possible, keep your focus on yourself. Break your own records every day. A runner is successful if he breaks his own record, even if he reaches last in the race.

14. Analyse your failure: Analyse every failure that you have faced. Think what was lacking and what was the mistake you made. If you carry out a proper analysis you will surely find some fault in your work or with your attitude.

15. Proper utilisation of resources: To become successful, whenever possible, make the maximum and optimum utilisation of resources with proper thinking, understanding, common sense, and patience.

If you attain the first step of success then make the effort to reach the second one, and be eager for the third step of success.

Life Means Moving On...

Moving on is life; stability or stagnancy is another name of death.

Mobility is everywhere, all around us. Ever notice the small creatures, animals, and birds? They are never inactive; they constantly remain busy in their work. They enjoy good health, beauty, and vigour due to their regular moving life.

A person who regularly uses his physical, mental, and spiritual powers remains younger and healthier longer. Non-working body parts degenerate and the result is a downfall in health, ugliness, and negativities in life. The short life of today's modern man is mainly due to his inactive and motionless life. They need conveyance even to travel small distances. Their sedentary lifestyles are causing their immune system to breakdown and invite innumerable diseases.

Moving on also means keeping yourself busy with something or the other in life. Avoid a life of laziness and dormancy.

Laziness is our enemy; activity is a symbol of awareness in life. Effort is man's most important wealth. A lazy person is an enemy of his family and the society. He spends his life on the collective labour of others. Every family should address this issue and try as far as possible to avoid it. It is the duty of the head of the family to make the children in the family active and find ways to keep them busy. Laziness in children can cause immense harm in their future life. The elders in the family should set a good example to their children by being active and busy in their work. They should always strive to complete the work undertaken and also give time to other interests. A family prospers when it works hard and works regularly. Being active produces a brilliant, healthy, and beautiful nature.

Passion

Short-term but deep interest in any work is called passion.

Any task to be successfully complete requires full dedication and a lot of passion, whether it is done by a commoner or a celebrity. It is only passion that gives all of the power to live our lives the way we want to live. People who lack passion, continue to blame various factors for their failures and unsatisfactory life style. They tend to depend on external factors to find happiness – promotions, desired bank balances, liberation from ailments and illnesses. What they fail to realise is that to find true happiness what is needed is a heart full of passion. To prosper in life use your passion; with it you can create anything, but without it you can lose everything. Passion helps you understand and search the deep meaning of your work and life.

Passion is a powerful instrument that can be used to become compatible with your conscience, and it is only your conscience that makes you active and helps you concentrate better and become tension-free.

Most people feel very enthused and excited about doing certain things in their lives, but when these things have to be done regularly, then these people become uninterested and at times negative too. So, to maintain passion in every single moment of your life, protect your passion. Use your passion to drive yourself to exceed your limited personal achievements; value it and it will become your self-motivator to stimulate you towards further growth and improvement. Discover your passion in life and live according to it. There is nothing more important that this in life.

Having The Safety Shield of Insurance

Insurance of two kinds: (1) Life insurance, (2) Non-life insurance.

(1) Life Insurance

The objective of life insurance is to provide financial security and income to the dependants of the bread winner of the family, in case of his untimely death.

Life insurance cannot protect the untimely death of a person but protects the family of the deceased by providing a financial shield. Life insurance is not an alternative to a person's death but is just another option of income.

Anything can happen to anyone, at any place, and at any time – untimely death, accident, loss of the ability to earn a living, illness, etc. If a husband wants that his wife remain independent after his death then he can make arrangements for huge amounts of money for his wife by buying her life insurance.

Parents dream big for their children's futures – education, marriage, later life, etc. Life insurance takes care of all this even if the parents are no more.

Life insurance also becomes extremely when people suddenly lose their job or families face financial crises.

That is why life insurance supports in both the situations – before death and after death.

How much insurance is enough for a person?

Try and get a cover that is at least twelve times that of your annual income.

If there are any unpaid loans, then add them into the total. If you have made any investments from which you receive a regular income, then subtract that amount from the total.

How much total amount will I get after maturity of my policy is that question that maximum people ask their insurance agents while buying a policy. Maximum people lose their sufficient life cover in order to gain huge amounts at the end of the term.

But the truth is that insurance and investments are two different issues. At the time of taking insurance, instead of expecting higher returns, it should be considered how much money that insurance policy will provide on the non-existence of that person. Term insurance is the best in that matter; it provides only life cover and does not provide any returns. That is why it is the cheapest. Sufficient insurance cover can be done easily.

After term insurance choose other options of insurance depending on your needs (children's education, marriage, etc.).

Buy insurance policies for the children

Many people buy insurance policies for their children. Generally, the object behind it is to collect money for expenditure that will be used for their education or marriage. Occasionally they forget that children don't bring income into the family. That is why the head of the family should first buy insurance cover for himself and then think of buying policies for his children. You can provide for the needs of your children by taking out payments from your investments.

Avoid the urge of taking less insurance cover

A lot of times people make the mistake of treating insurance as just a medium of tax saving. To save tax from being deducted they only pay that much premium that will save their tax, without caring much about how less the amount of insurance cover is.

Some people consider life insurance a waste of money.

Their idea is: what is the use of receiving money after death. What they fail to see is how the insurance money becomes a source of income and is a security for their family. Financial experts are of the view that a person should give first priority to his life insurance among all the other important things such as bank savings, investments, insurance, and Mediclaim.

Other benefits of life insurance

1. Taking life insurance policy along with a loan, gives a person the freedom of not paying back the loan amount to his family members on his sudden death.
2. In old age the maturity amount of the policy becomes a source of regular income for the aged couple.
3. Sometimes business organisations may have to face a big loss due to the sudden death of its important person. The organisation may have taken many loans. To avoid such a situation, a keyman policy can be taken. The key person may be the owner or even an employee of the organisation.
4. Many people want to continue to contribute towards society even after they have finally departed from the world. Such people can assign a good amount policy to some trust. With the regular income of this amount, charitable work can continue forever.
5. Life insurance serves as a protection and safeguard against emergencies in life. Senior citizens can leave behind this protection for their children even if they do not have other assets to distribute to their children.
6. Some riders can be taken along with a regular life insurance policy, such as critical illness, etc.

That is why people should accept life insurance with desire and should ask for it.

Keep in mind the following:

1. Life insurance can be taken only till one's health is fit. That is why this very essential task should not be delayed or kept to be done in old age.
2. Life insurance should be taken at an early age because sudden death in an early age tends to create more problems for the family. By buying an insurance at an early age, less premium has to be paid. It is better to take a long-term insurance at an early age, because as the age increases the premium too keeps on increasing and the clauses related to health also start becoming tough to satisfy.
3. Review your insurance after every one or two years, because it is possible that during this period your personal situation, income, assets, and liabilities have changed.
4. Some companies give life insurance coverage to their employees. Nowadays, especially for youngsters, changing jobs has become a common practice; in such a situation is it not wise to depend on your organisation for your insurance-related security. It could also be possible that the insurance cover being provided by your employer is not enough for you. Thus, one should also take additional insurance according to your needs.
5. Never forget to deposit premium instalments on time.

Non-Life Insurance (General Insurance)

In non-life insurance there are many types of coverage available – natural adversities, such as floods, earthquakes, dust-storms, windstorms, etc.; losses incurred due to them can be covered by insurance.

Business families can provide security to their business by buying insurance coverage of fire, riots, etc.

In the same way shopkeepers' insurance policy can be taken for the security of the shop.

People engaged in farming can secure their crops by buying climate or crop insurance.

In the same way vehicle insurance can be taken, in which at least third party insurance is compulsory by law.

Some important Indian insurance policies

Health Insurance (Mediclaim Policy)

Many people who don't take a mediclaim policy cover, end up borrowing either large sums of money or selling away their assets in order to meet hospital expenses.

Happiness can only be attained, when there is a provision to meet your medical expenses, and in this matter mediclaim insurance can become your biggest support.

Though an employee has health insurance covered by his organisation he should take additional health insurance due to his frequent job changes.

Personal Accidental Plan

The danger of a youngster dying or becoming handicapped due to some accident is more than him dying a natural death. We read about youngsters dying in accidents almost every day in the newspapers. Obviously the youngsters face the danger of accident much more than people who are aged. To save one's self from the danger of being handicapped and becoming dependent on someone, insurance companies offer personal accident cover along with disability cover. The insurance premium of such policies is very less.

The following things are covered in such policies:

Death: The nominee gets the insurance amount only after the death of the policy holder.

Permanent total disability: The full insurance amount is paid if some permanent total disability occurs, such as the damage of eyes, loss of limbs, etc.

Permanent partial disability: The claim is settled on that percentage which is mentioned in the policy. It depends on the type of disability — loss of a finger, loss of an eye, etc.

Temporary total disability: Claim will be settled on the basis of disability – getting a fracture.

Loss-of-income rider: After an accident, a person may not be able to attend his office due to temporary disability and his income stops for some time. In such a condition, if he has bought the loss-of-income rider then the insurance company provides him an income on a weekly basis.

Home Insurance

Incidents are out of our control. There may be earthquakes, floods, fires, burglaries, and house breaking that may result in a loss of our properties and homes. Loss related to home hurt people deeply. No one can compensate emotional losses, but in this unfortunate condition home insurance can provide relief from financial losses.

In situation of losses due to internal fire, blast, earthquake, house struck by lightening, thunderstorm, flood, gas leakage, leakage of water tank or pipes, burglary and house breaking, loss due to some vehicle, etc., a person can get insurance money through structural insurance.

In this the reinstatement of the house is provided. This insurance is also quite reasonable.

Content insurance policy gives insurance safety to things kept in your house. In this policy along with natural climatic disasters, losses that occur due to social evils such as burglary and house breaking are also compensated.

Loss of electric and electronic items, furniture and fixtures, clothes, jewellery, and expensive precious stones, etc., can also be covered by getting them insured.

Insurance agent: He is your good friend and also your family's.

As soldiers protect the nation, insurance agents helps in building the nation.

Just as a doctor helps you in treating your disease and an advocate helps you in settling disputes, your insurance agent guides you and informs you how to financially secure your future.

Every family these days has a family doctor or a family lawyer; in the same way adopt an insurance agent as your family friend.

He will fulfil his duties of friendship for many of your generations.

He will give you relevant information from time to time, provide suggestions to you, and contribute his services for life.

The Necessity of Nomination

What is nomination

Nomination is a convenience provided by banks and insurance companies under which an investor can nominate his successor, who is eligible to claim the invested amount after the death of the investor. A nominee can be appointed for all such assets on which you have ownership rights. This includes fixed deposits, insurance policies, mutual funds, provident funds, PPF, real estate, and shares in DEMAT accounts.

For a person to be eligible for nomination, he should be aged 18 years or more. If a nominee is not a major, then an appointee has to be mentioned. The name of a nominee can be changed at any time and renewed.

Funds are easily released if there is a nominee

If any person has mentioned a nominee then after his death his assets can easily be transferred to his nominee. For this, the nominee has to submit a death certificate of the deceased and make some important declarations on a form. Once this is complete the assets of the deceased can be claimed.

Process will be completed in case of no nomination

If a person passes away without making any nomination then it becomes very difficult for the family members to claim the assets. However, the RBI has now made this process quite simple in comparison to the earlier process.

If there is no nomination then after the death of depositor, his family members have to submit death certificate along with affidavit, in which all the successors of the expired person are mentioned and their consent is taken for transfer of assets.

In many cases succession certificate is required. For this an application in court has to be submitted, in which all the details of the successors of the deceased person is to be mentioned. After that regarding this a notice is published in newspaper. If no objection is received in connection to this notice then court passes succession certificate. Generally, too much time is taken for this process to complete.

When to nominate

1. At the time of investment/deposits.
2. After marriage, to nominate your partner in the previous deposits.
3. If the nominated person passes away then a new nominee has to be mentioned.
4. There is no nomination in the insurance policies of children; nominations should be done as soon as they become adults.
5. Nomination of insurance policies becomes void when receiving loans from banks. But once the policy is released from mortgage, immediately get a new nomination done. If the circumstances of the earlier nomination change, it is required to renew the nomination.

Good Salesman

Products are produced to be sold to the consumers. The companies producing the goods become secondary in the consumer market because it is the salesperson who takes the first place. A salesman is the actual rower of the industrial boat. He knows the art of selling, and an expert salesman can sell snow to an Eskimo."Who so ever sells is brave". Such a person is valuable for selling any product and so he should be taken care of. He should be given good remuneration, respect, honour, and comfortable facilities. The following story explains the qualities that a perfect salesman should have.

This is the story of a boy who went for an interview but got rejected because he was unable to speak properly in English. But the boy did not give up. He confronted the manager and asked to be given a chance a proving himself, because it was his selling skills that were being put to test, not his command over the English language. The manager was pleased with this proposal and the boy was taken on board. After the boy joined the store, the sales of the store began increasing manifolds. When the owner got to know about this he was curious to meet this boy and watch him at work. So, one day he walked in and found the boy selling a fishing rod to a customer. As the owner stood and watched amazed, the boy convinced the customer to buy a pair of fishing shoes, because the ones that he was wearing were too expensive to be worn during fishing. Once the customer bought the shoes, the boy reminded him that he would be sitting in the sun, and waiting for hours to catch the fish. So the customer bought a hat and some food stuff. The boy then sold him a basket in which he could carry his food. By now the customer's bill was huge and so were the sales figures. After watching and listening to the entire conversation between the boy and the customer, the owner was extremely impressed and congratulated the boy on the good sales that he had done. To this the boy explained to the owner that the customer had actually come to buy some sanitary napkins. Seeking the opportunity, the boy suggested that the customer go fishing instead of sitting at home for the next four days.

An expert salesman creates requirements of the customers and fulfils them by his products.

It is very important for a salesman to ask for the order. Many sales are lost and damaged if the salesman is shy in asking for orders.

For the salesman there is only one target — that although many people may say "no" to buying the product, but someone will say "yes".

It is very important for a good salesman to understand the requirements of his customer.

What People Want

Selling is fun and simple. It is merely finding out what people want and showing them how they can get it from you.

People want to gain:

Health, wealth, benefits from good opportunities, pleasures and amenities, popularity, better appearance, and status.

People want to be:

Good parents, good hosts, influential, and expert at working

People want to:

Express themselves, satisfy their curiosities and eagerness, acquire material things, copy personalities, and try to move ahead of the other person.

People want to save:

Time, wealth and, their health.

People want to avoid:

Hard work, troubles and pains, stressful situations, risks, and from being insulted.

Selling begins with identifying what the customer wants.

Win The Customer

Try and find out why your customers are decreasing. Could it be because of one of the following?

1% passed away

2% changed city

5% made new relations

14% got dissatisfied by the product

68% get annoyed by the careless behaviour of someone in your organisation

Try and analyse the reason why your customers have decreased and learn some new ways to make them loyal to you. When a businessman or shopkeeper displays a good behaviour to his customers then he makes them his customers forever. Good behaviour here means talking politely, using kind and sweet language to address the customer, and adopting a good culture. Wherever and whenever a customer gets importance and respect, good and transparent service, and a good product at a good price he will continue to return to that place. In any type of business, "to know the requirements of the customer and to fulfil them" is the key to success. It would be useful to remember some of the following:

Customers are never an inconvenience; they are the businessman's bread and butter.

Customer is the boss whom you always have to keep happy.

Customer has a requirement and it has to be fulfilled.

Customer has feelings and they have to be taken care of.

Customer is always in a "hurry"; his work should be taken care of immediately.

Tackle difficult customers cautiously and with sympathy. Place yourself in their position and understand their problem; try and get rid of their irritation by rectifying their problems and bring a smile on their face.

If a customer goes back happy and satisfied then he will come back with more customers.

To retain your customers, always provide them the best after-sale services according to their needs.

Financial Planning

Financial planning allows us to systematically manage our finance and financial assets; this proper management later fulfils the objectives of our life.

There is no doubt that it takes single drops of water to fill a pot and the same drops one by one can also empty it. So, it is essential that you carry out the proper accounting of your income and expenditure, so that you how much you have earned and how much you have spent.

Always make a budget depending on your expected income.

Avoid wasting money and try to always carry out its proper utilisation according to your needs at that time; whenever possible save the balance money.

Keep Savings

Generally we make budgets for our expenses, but do not think enough about savings. A change is required in this type of thinking; it should be realised that planning for savings is also necessary.

You can't be prosperous by neglecting savings.

If you spend first and save the rest then you will be able to save only very little. If you first save and then spend the rest, then you won't face major problems in attaining your financial goals. If you adopt this as your habit, then you will save a good amount in a long period.

Children should be encouraged to save, otherwise their habits are spoilt by spending more than what is required.

It is not necessary to deposit huge or big amounts of money for saving. Even if a small amount is deposited from time to time regularly then it will continue to increase in due course of time.

It is not important how much you earn, but it is extremely important how much you save, because however high a person's income may be, he will be in trouble if he is spending more than his income. In the same way however less the income of a person may be, if his expenditure is less than his income he will always be happy.

Adopt a balanced attitude towards savings. Do not save so much that in trying to make beautiful arrangements for your future you start facing problems in the present. But the reverse is also true. Also, don't spend so much in entertainment and in buying yourself fancy things that you forget about your future.

Save at least 30 percent of your income so that you may fulfil your needs in the future.

(A lot of money can be saved by stopping extravagant expenditure).

Extravagance

People who are used to extravagance and unnecessary expenses, are unable to cope up with their expenses even when they earn a good income. They try to spend on every single object that fascinates their innumerable desires. Majority of such people who do this do not know the difference between desires and necessary requirements. Requirements get fulfilled some time or the other but desires have no limits. Extravagance can make people criminals.

In cities there is always an undesirable tendency of pomp and show and false splendour. You can see that on roads, streets, in parks, in temples, and the maximum during marriage ceremonies. Perhaps pomp and show of dresses and grace are the maximum – uncontrollable desire in the youth to decorate themselves and to get dressed in the best way. People spend more than their income to display their wealth to others and as a result face undesirable results like business-related insolvency, numerous court cases of fraud, different kinds of crimes, in which people get severe punishments for dishonesty and cheating.

Numerous people, even though educated, also get caught in the web of debt, unhappiness, helplessness, suicide, excitement, crime, and corruption.

By using electricity, gas, petrol wisely, extravagant expenditure can be avoided on them. Junk food, smoking, drinking, etc., that are harmful for health should be cut down and as a result of which extravagant expenditure will also stop. Intelligently spend only on those things that are useful for you.

If you stick to only using your debit card instead of your credit card then you can avoid purchasing things that are of no importance to you.

In any condition, as far as possible, avoid taking loans. Problems start when you are unable to pay the loan back due to whatever reason. Make a target to be loan-free in life.

Firm Source of Income After Retirement

Whenever we think about our life after retirement then a certain picture develops in our minds – a stable and calm life after the helter and skelter life of the younger years. A life that can be lived peacefully and a life in which you have as much money so that you can spend comfortably for the rest of your days.

Hence, start saving plans right now, while you can, for your retirement funds.

For this you can deposit in Public Provident Fund (PPF). A PPF account can be opened at the post office or State Bank of India or some other specific banks. You can deposit up to Rs. one lakh tax-free in a year in this account. You don't have to pay tax on the interest earned from this investment.

It helps to start depositing at an early age. Try and understand this from the following example:

First stage: If you start depositing Rs. 100,000 per year for ten years starting at an age of 21 then by the age of 65 it will become approximately 2 crores and 45 lakhs.

Second stage: If you invest Rs. 100,000 per year starting from the age of 31 for 35 years means till the age of 65, it will become approximately 1 crore 83 lakhs till the age of 65.

Third stage: If you deposit Rs. 100,000 per year from the age of 21 for 45 years means till the age of 65, then your savings will be approximately 4 crores 29 lakhs till the age of 65.

It is clear from the above three stages that as you start saving at a very early age you can get accordingly huge amounts of money at the time of your retirement. At an early age expenses are also less, so savings can be done easily. Other than the PPF, many other saving plans can also be opted for.

At least 10 percent of our income should be invested in your retirement fund for a comfortable retirement.

Our biggest mistake is withdrawing and using that fund before retirement. By not using this fund, we can enjoy rest of our life with income from this fund after retirement.

Remember

Out of those people who start their career at an age of 25 and continue till the age of 65:

1% people are rich and wealthy.

4% people are self dependent.

5% people are still working.

36% people are dead.

54% people are dependent.

To live dependent is like living your life in hell.

Set target: Set your medium- and long-term goals. After how many years you have to purchase your own house, after how many days you have to increase the size of your family, quality education to be given to your children, purchasing your car, etc., may be all the targets that change from family to family. After setting your goals it is important to decide how much you have to keep on investing to attain these goals.

Investment: With the guarantee of a secure future and to fulfil the requirement of time to time, investment becomes a source of regular income.

For savings, invest money in different plans. You can get the benefit from schemes offered by post offices and banks.

You can also choose from other attractive options of investments from where you can get best safe returns; they can be chosen for investing. Decide intelligently in the matter of investments. Whichever option you choose, it should be according to your requirements. In this matter, your requirements depend on your age, financial resources, risk profile, objectives of your investment, etc. At the time of buying an investment plan, keep in mind how much return you are expecting and after how much time it will be returned.

Share Market/Mutual Fund

To get fast and huge profits a large number of people put their money in share market.

Any intelligent investor has knowledge of basic principles of investment in the share market. The principle is that buy at a lower rate and sell it at a higher rate, but sometimes people are carried away by the sentiments of the market. Positive sentiments dominate when the market is rising. People make investments in this situation so that they don't miss the opportunity to gain the accruing profit. The reverse of it is when the market is on a downfall; then the sentiments are negative and people become hesitant of the approaching loses and start selling their shares. When the market is on a rise that is the time to sell rather than purchase; in the same way, it is sensible to purchase on a downward trend rather than sell.

To avoid such situations, divide your investments: invest half in the share market and half in buying instruments that give fixed income. Whenever there is a rise and fall in the market than do the valuation of both and make them equal. This means, if the value of portfolio shares is on the higher side then transfer some funds to the fixed income portfolio, and if the value of the portfolio of shares has fallen then transfer some funds from the fixed income portfolio to the share market portfolio.

Invest your money for the long term and avoid the delusion of taking account of your money daily. Carrying out day trading is not possible by everyone.

The worst thing is to investment in shares by taking a loan. When the market reverses, then these are the people who become troubled first. No matter what, avoid this indulgence.

Importance of insurance

Many people think insurance is not that important and consider it an unnecessary expenditure. This is foolish thinking. Insurance is compulsory for everyone. If you have a family (husband/wife, children, parents, etc.) then it becomes even more compulsory. In the situation of any sudden unforeseen incident, life insurance becomes a big support for your family.

In the same way health insurance is also compulsory. By virtue of this, at the time of illness you can ascertain arrangements for your or your family's treatment.

Accidental insurance too also equally important.

If sufficient insurance is not bought then your total budget gets disturbed in an emergency situation. Take care of your future by acting now.

Emergency fund

To fulfil requirements of three to six months you should always have some liquidity funds put away so that they be used as emergency expenditures.

Inflation: If we pay attention to the ever-rising inflation then it becomes important to increase savings and decrease extravagant expenditures.

Take a look at the following. Where we spend 100 rupees today:

After 10 years Rs. 260 will be required.

After 20 years Rs. 673 will be required.

After 30 years Rs. 1745 will be required.

After 40 years Rs. 4525 will be required.

After 50 years Rs. 11740 will be required.

If we keep our savings locked in at home, its value will keep on decreasing due to the inflation, hence it is important to invest this amount.

Balance sheet

It is important to regularly make yearly or half-yearly balance sheets of your assets and liabilities. Your net wealth will the amount left after deducting liabilities from your assets.

If the amount that is derived after adding the GDP rate or interest rate and the inflation rate on last years' wealth, is more than this year's wealth then we are reducing wealth; if it is equal then we are saving nothing; and if it is less then we are saving properly.

Remember

1. To increase income we should not depend on one source. At least two sources should be there. If there is a problem in one then we can depend on the second one. Think of discarding the old source only when a new source has been established and is dependable.
2. Investments should be made in the name of both the spouses, jointly on either or survivor basis, so that in the absence of one, the other can withdraw.
3. Make nominations in all the investments.
4. Definitely make your will.
5. Maintain detailed records of your investments.

Make all members of your family self-dependent.

Make Your Will

What Is A "Will"

A "will" is the legal statement of a person's wishes concerning the disposal of his property and assets after his death. A will ascertains your intentions of who should get your property after your death.

The person making the will can give his wealth to his children, relatives, friends, some trust, his servants, or to whomsoever he wants and feels fit.

A will comes into effect only after the death of the person who made the will.

A will can be changed and altered at any time in life before one's death. It can also be modified and revoked.

A person can make his will any number of times, but it is the last will made before one's death that holds true and is the one applicable.

No law can change the will of a person after his death.

Who can make a will

Any adult who is mentally fit can get a will made. Handicapped and illiterate people can also make a will. Women too have the power to have their will made of their self-earned wealth, presents, items of her dowry, or her personal property (*stridhan*). Only self-earned wealth can be distributed by way of a will.

A will made under the influence of intoxicants, or made forcefully or by unlawful means is not valid, because such a will does not express the self-desire of the person making the will.

When is the right time to get a will made

A will can be made at any time during one's life, but it is better if it is done on time, especially if one is married and has family. Married partners should prepare separate wills.

Why is a will important

Family disputes

Without 'Will' any unknown person may take possession on the property.

Benefits of having a will

After death the possibility of dispute is negated and the property is divided as per the will. A will is a valid document according to the law and it is applicable everywhere including the court. It is a confidential document that only the will holder is aware about.

Though you distribute your property through your will, but the powers still remain with you. You can utilise the property as per your desire at any time during your lifetime. This way you will never be dependent on others.

You have full right on the property acquired by you. To distribute it between your children or not, is your personal decision. You may divide it the way you wish. For instance, if you think your daughter-in-law deserves the property more than your son, you must go ahead and give it to her. The point is that the property that you have acquired with your hard work should not go to waste after your death.

A will is the final document that is used for the distribution of the wealth of the deceased. You may have made your children as your nominee in your land property, bank accounts, insurance policies, or other shares, but the nominee is not the final owner or heir. A nominee can be regarded as the heir or owner only if the same is also mentioned in the will. If a person is not a nominee, but has been named in the will, then he will be treated as the final owner.

A will is a legal document that should be made by everyone. It is not true that a will is required by only those people who hold large amounts of property and wealth, and that they make a will because after their death they want to avoid disputes among their children. A will should be treated as a document of your last desire. Maybe that is why in Hindi it is called *Ichchapatra* (desired letter).

Other benefits

1. Any property attained through a will does not attract any stamp duty.
2. If any wealth is acquired through a will, then there is no transfer capital gain and no gift tax is imposed on it.
3. Through a will, wealth can be distributed to children's H.U.F. By this way a different H.U.F. can be made for these children. A good tax planning can be done by making their H.U.F.
4. Any trust can be made through your will and the income from that trust can be provided to anybody, as per the wish of the person making that will; this way by making a trust, tax savings can also be done.

Why to make a will

The process of making a will is really easy. A will does not have any regular form. It can even be written on a simple sheet of paper. A self-hand written will is the best.

Stamp duty is not compulsory. To make a will no lawyer is required, but it is better to consult an intellectual person.

A will can be made in any language but a will should always be made in a language that the person making the will can read and understand properly.

There is no need for you to use any heavy legal terminology or technical words in your will. Write in clear and simple words. If you keep your words unclear then your objective may not get fulfilled.

Select all your words properly and write them in the proper context.

Never use nicknames or incomplete names in your will.

Write clearly about the beneficiary to whom you are assigning your property. Do clearly mention the name, father's name, address, and your relation with the person.

It is not compulsory that you give the entire portion of your property to your near and dear ones. If you want to assign part or even the full portion of your property to someone else, who is more close and loving to you, it is allowed under the law. But for this to hold true, it is important that the same is mentioned clearly in your will.

If a person making the will does not want a particular person to be part of his will and knows that after his death this person can present a claim on the wealth, then in such a situation it is important that the person making the will clarify the reason for not making that particular person a shareholder in the total wealth.

To avoid a dispute from arising on any part of your wealth that is not mentioned in the will, one should make a will of his full wealth. If you hold a joint property with a partner, then the will can include only that portion of the property that is under your name. A partner possesses the rights of making the will of the portion of property that is with the partner. If both have equal portions then one partner can make the will only for that 50% portion of his property.

All provisions made in the will should be in the context of that property, such as:

- Self-earned movable property such as cash, household items, jewellery, money deposited in banks, provident fund, shares, partnership in any company, etc.
- Self-earned immovable property such as land, house, shop, farmland, etc.
- Any ancestral property may be movable or unmovable that is in your name. For that, full description of the property, the means of possessing it, and its approximate value is written.

- The person making the will should write in the will that he is making the will in his full senses and that his mental status is healthy and stable. Own educational qualifications should also be mentioned.

Make sure to mention the date while writing your will.

It should also be written in the will that "before this date any previous will stands null and void".

Sign on every page of your will in the presence of two witnesses. The witnesses should also write their full name and address on the will and sign it. It is better to put thumb impressions of the witnesses and your own. The age of the witnesses should be less than the person making the will.

Such a person cannot become a witness who is a beneficiary in the will. The witness should not be benefitted by any way, directly or indirectly, through the will.

While signing the will the witness should be in his senses and his mental status should be perfect.

An ideal situation is if out of both the witnesses one is a doctor and the other is a lawyer. The presence of a doctor justifies that the person making the will was in his full senses and was mentally fit at the time of making the will. The presence of a lawyer makes it clear that the person making the will has sought legal advice.

Number each page of the will and mention the total number of pages at the end.

It is better to have a video recording of the entire process of making the will, though it is not mandatory by law.

The registration of a will is not mandatory but if required it can be registered at a sub-registrar's office. If at any time the person making the will wants to withdraw his will then he can do so.

In any sort of a judicial obstacle, a registered will has more importance.

The biggest benefit of getting the will registered is that once it has been registered it goes into the safe custody of the registrar. No tampering can happen with it, and neither can it be destroyed or stolen.

You, yourself can get your will registered at the registrar's office.

The registration fee is very nominal.

While making a will make more than one copy. At least one copy should be with your most confidential person so that it can be utilised in difficult situations.

Precautions

If at the time of making the will it is difficult to make a proper or even distribution of the wealth, then the person making the will can purchase his life insurance policy and include it to have proper distribution of his wealth.

Many times it has been seen that husbands in their will distribute their wealth in the name of their children. This is not reasonable, because if the wife inherits nothing how is she supposed to take care of the kids and herself in the absence of her husband?. The logical solution is that both the husband and wife should make separate wills of the wealth that they own personally. The will and its contents should remain confidential. If disclosed, it may result in undesirable consequences.

It is a good idea to keep updating your will from time to time.

To appoint executor

Most experts have a common view that an executor should be appointed by a person for his will. An executor is a person, who sees to it that your wishes as per your will are carried out after your death. It is very important that you mention the name of an executor in your will. If there is no name of an executor in the will, then the court may appoint an administrator to fulfil this duty.

Will and probate

A certified copy issued by the court is called a probate.

To probate means to prove authentication of a will. It also means to prove that the will is real or false. This is required when someone presents an objection against the will.

What if a will is not made

If a person has not made his will then property of the deceased is divided between the family members of the deceased in accordance to the successors.

According to the law of succession, if a person dies without making a will, then his property is distributed equally among his legal successors.

Under the succession act, there are about 8 categories of successors. On the basis of these categories, different people of the family are included. In accordance of these categories, claims can be put up for the property of the deceased . The first right is of class-1 successors; if there is no one to make a claim in it then class-2 comes into consideration. If still there is no one to make claim then class-3 comes into consideration. In the same way further categories are considered. On the basis of religion, the law of succession is different in different religions.

Terminology attached to the process of making a will

Testator: Testator is the person who makes the will; it means the person who signs on the will.

Legatees or Beneficiary: This is the person whose name is being mentioned in the will. Those people to whom the wealth is given in the will are called beneficiaries.

Codisil: Once a will is made and later some changes are made in it, after that these changes are called codisil.

Distribution: To distribute property.

Executor: The person making the will entrusts it to a confidential person. This person after the death of the testator then reads the will to the family of the testator. This person is known as an executor.

Bequest: Document of will.

Testament: Document of will.

Will: Desired letter.

Legacy: Property left behind by the deceased.

Green Living

There is a deep relationship between the environment and human life. Both influence each other. Human life develops well within a clean and pure environment, but when the environment becomes polluted it causes diseases and different types of mental and physical disorders and human life is degraded. Environmental pollution is the main cause of diseases.

Because nowadays trees, plants, parks, forests, green areas, etc., have reduced, the environment is under threat and all sorts of environmental imbalances are occurring.

All living beings take in food and oxygen and give out carbon dioxide.

$C_6H_{12}O_6 + 6O_2 = 6\ CO_2 + 6\ H_2O + \text{Energy}$

Glucose (food) + Oxygen = Carbon dioxide+ water + energy.

Trees and plants takes in carbon dioxide and provide food and oxygen.

$6\ CO_2 + 6\ H_2O + \text{Solar Energy} = C_6H_{12}O_6 + 6\ O_2$

Carbon dioxide+water+solar energy=glucose (food)+oxygen.

In this way the environmental balance is maintained. Hence, all of us should plant trees on a large scale around us.

Trees and plants are also used

1. As fuel to cook food
2. To produce water by protecting the moisture
3. As food items
4. To provide fibres, such as cotton, jute, flax, etc., to make cloth

5. As wood for houses and on farms
6. As medicinal herbs for the treatment of illnesses
7. As fodder for domesticated animals
8. To produce flowers for the floriculture industry
9. To provide shelter and beautification
10. To produce rains

There is no part of a tree that does not come in use in some way or the other.

Popular shady trees include *peepal*, banyan, *mahua*, mango, and neem tree. These trees are not only big in size, but they also have long lives. Much importance is given to plant these trees because of the benefits they enjoy. Farmers plant them in their farms and farmlands so that they can make their huts beneath them to live in. In villages, under these huge-sized trees *gram panchayats* as well as social get-togethers, such as marriage functions, festivals, etc., are held. They also prove as good shelters for animals and birds.

Neem

The neem is supposed to be the most beneficial among the trees mentioned earlier. In our country it is one of the most important resources of medication and is used in farming purposes too. Neem trees provide dense greenery and shelter; they have no danger of wood worms or white ants. There is immense power in every part of a neem tree for curing diseases.

Mango

Everybody is familiar with mango. In India it is the king of all fruits. Its wood is used in ritual ceremonies (*havan*) as a burning agent.

Mahua

Mahua is also a useful tree like the mango. By planting some plants of these, people in rural areas use it to earn their livelihood. The flowers and seeds of the mahua are more useful than the fruit of the mango tree. In hilly regions uncivilised tribes depend on the mahua plant to fulfil more then half their requirements of grains; this is done by drying the mahua flower.

Peepal

The shelter of a peepal tree creates a healthy atmosphere. Its regular use reduces *vata* (gas), *pitta* (acid), and *kapha* (cough).

Banyan Tree

The shelter of a banyan tree provides a miraculous atmosphere for meditation and communion (*samadhi*).

Plants and trees are also auspicious

A lot of us for the fulfilment of our various desires and for countering the evil planetary effects wear precious stones, such as emerald (*panna*), coral (*munga*), topaz (*pukhraj*), sapphire (*neelam*), etc. These precious stones are not only very expensive but also very difficult to differentiate between real and fake by a common person. A simple and cheap alternative is also present in our ancient holy books. By planting some special trees we can get the same type of benefits that we get by wearing these precious stones.

Basil

This is a life-giving plant. This should be kept in the house. This plant wards off inauspicious energy, and cleans and purifies polluted air. Its consumption is helpful in many diseases.

Banana

It is auspicious to plant a banana tree within the boundary of a house. It is more auspicious to plant it in the north-east area of the house. By placing a pot of basil plant near a banana tree, structural defects (*vastu dosha*) can be overcome.

Ashwagandha

A plant of ashwagandha growing by itself within the boundary of house, is very auspicious and good for eliminating *vastu* faults. It is also a medicinal plant.

Wood Apple (*bail*)

A wood apple tree within the boundary walls of a house is supposed to be the most auspicious. Our ancient mythologies mention that the house in which Lord Shiva's most loving wood apple tree exists, Lakshmi ji the Goddess of money and wealth reside at that place for generations.

Coconut

According to *vastu granthas*, the existence of a coconut tree within the boundary of a house is also very auspicious. By its presence people living in that house receive respect and honour as well as progress rapidly in their life.

Gulmohar

A gulmohar tree planted anywhere near the house is supposed to be best for its auspicious effect. By the end of the spring, the tree bears red flowers. The air from the gulmohar tree is supposed to work as oxygen for ailing people.

Ashoka

By planting the ashoka tree near the house, faults of any inauspicious energy are removed.

Tree planting is not only beneficial for the person planting it, but it also benefits the entire human community.

Every person should plant and protect at least five plants in his life.

Children should be encouraged to cultivate the habit of planting trees and plants during their holidays. Children enjoy when they see the plants or trees planted by them growing.

Recognise the importance and utilities of trees. Planting of trees should be understood as religious work, social responsibility, family's ritual ceremony, and personal responsibility.

Where to plant

In the house-courtyard, terrace-roof, kitchen garden, any place that you think fit can be turned into a garden. We can grow fresh fruits and vegetables at the same time also reap the emotional benefits of caring for the plants.

It is not important that trees should be planted inside the house. They can be planted anywhere nearby where they can be properly cared and looked after by the person planting them.

They can also be planted alongside roads and highways, on river banks, near temples, in schools, in parks, etc. Basically, our cities and towns need to go green.

Love For The Nation

The greatest mark of national love is to obey the law and order of your country.

Putting up industry is also national love

He who puts his money and establishes an industry is also a nation lover. He takes a risk and provides shape to an industry, by his hard work so that hundreds and thousands of people can get employment. Hence, starting up industries gives new life to industries.

To save wastage is also national love

Every day all around us we see the extensive wastage of water. Not only is water uselessly wasted, but also the same is done with electricity and fuel. Our attitude is such that we don't think we are wasting these utilities. Neither do we realise that our wastage of such valuable resources actually deprives others of them.

If we save these resources, we not only save our own money but also save the valuable resources of our country.

Save water, save the environment

Today almost all countries are facing the problem of water scarcity. If we don't save water today then there will be a day when we will be fighting wars over water.

- Don't keep the tap running while brushing your teeth, shaving, or washing the utensils. Make it a habit to close the water tap when it is not being used.

- Instead of washing your car using a garden hose wash your car with water from a bucket. Immediately repair any point of leakage in your house. Instead of using outdated flush toilets, get the latest water-saver toilets fitted in your washrooms.

- Don't waste water that is discharged from your A.C., R.O., and other such gadgets. Conserve it and use it to clean floors or use it for watering plants in your garden. Water your plants in such a way that the water goes in the plants and pots only and is not spilled on the roads and drains, etc.

Save Electricity

Across our country and in the world there is acute energy crisis. The demand of electricity is much higher than its supply. So, we should use it intelligently.

There is major damage to the environment in the process of making electricity. So, by saving electricity you are also doing a favour to the environment around you.

Lighting system

- Switch off the lights and fans when they are not being used. As far as possible, use task lighting, which focuses light where it's needed. By this electricity will be consumed less.
- Clean tube lights and bulbs etc., regularly because being dirty they emit out 50% less lights.
- Use energy-efficient compact fluorescent lamps (CFL) in place of ordinary bulbs; they reduce energy consumption by up to 70%. Start using fluorescent bulbs because they consume 10–15% less electricity than ordinary bulbs.

Air conditioner

- Set the thermostat of your air conditioners at 25°C, so that the maximum benefit is gained with minimum costing.
- Keep doors closed of air conditioned room.

- Clean filters of air condition every month.
- Keep cut-off temperature of air condition on higher side and when not in use it should be switched off.
- Don't use air conditioners the entire night. The room gets cooled after a few hours of air condition being switched on. After that only the fan is enough to keep the room cool.
- If you are living on the top floor and using an air conditioner, then don't switch on the ceiling fan. The fan will throw hot air downwards and this will increase the load on the air conditioner.
- Try not to install your air conditioner on the west or south-west wall at the time of installation. This will help you save electricity.
- Take care that sunlight does not fall directly on the refrigerator and that no other type of warmth is reaching the fridge.
- Keep some space all around the fridge so that proper circulation of air may take place. Remember that if hot air is not exited properly, than the cooling system has to work more and electric consumption increased. In a manual defrost refrigerator, the freezer should be set to defrost regularly.
- Don't keep the doors of your refrigerator open for a long time.
- Regularly check the gasket of your fridge (rubber lining door).
- Keep things covered in the fridge. Uncovered things develop moisture, and that puts additional load on the fridge.

- Don't open the door of the fridge again and again. If there is a temperature regulator, then set the temperature of the refrigerator between 35° and 37° C and of the freezer to about 3°C.
- Don't put freshly baked or hot items straight into the fridge. Let them cool outside for about 10–15 minutes.

Invertor/generator

- Get one total installation relay for invertor/generator, so that your electricity meter doesn't run even during power cuts.

Microwave

- Use a microwave oven in place of an ordinary oven. This way up to 50% can be saved on your electricity expenses.
- Big and thick items should be kept on the outer edge because a microwave starts cooking things from the outer edges moving gradually towards the centre.

Computer

- When not in use, computers should be switched off.
- Also, screen savers do not save any energy.
- Monitors consume more than half of the total electricity; that is why if the computer has to be kept on, the monitor should be switched off.

Miscellaneous

- Charger/battery of mobile cameras or laptops when not required, their plugs should be removed from the sockets.

Note: Don't keep electronic items in sleep mode, because your electric meter records such consumptions.

Save Fuel (Petrol)

- Petrol and diesel harm the environment in a big way.
- Switch off the engine of your vehicle at red lights. By switching off your engine for about one to two minutes, you can save many litres of fuel in a month. In the same way keep your engine switched off when stuck in traffic jams or when waiting for someone.
- Get your vehicle serviced regularly and also get you're your pollution check done regularly. This way not only will you save petrol but you will also prevent air pollution from spreading.
- Don't drive your vehicle too fast or too slow; it reduces the average. Whereas the average gets better when the vehicle is driven at a constant speed.
- If you keep the machine of your vehicle clean, then 7 to 8 percent of your fuel can be saved in a month.
- Whenever possible, make use of car-pools instead of driving alone to the office. In the end, five people can reach their office at the same cost that you alone would have spent to go to the office.
- Don't use your car for small distances. Sometimes you should walk also. That way you save petrol and better your health. Also not using your car puts less pressure on the already heavy traffic.
- If you like you can also cycle down to some of the places you need to visit.

Save Paper

- Remember, 17 trees are cut off for 1 ton paper.
- Use both sides of a sheet of paper. This straightaway means decreasing the cutting down of trees by half.

- Make note pads of single-sided printed papers. Most of us do this at office but it helps if we continue to do it at home too. Use this practice at home to write your grocery lists, do rough calculations, or write reminders to yourself.
- Rather than throwing away used envelopes, folders, paper clips, and other stationery items, re-use them.
- Cut down the use of paper by noting things on computers, mobiles, emails, or digital diaries.
- Take a final print only once rather than taking prints again and again. If possible, take prints in small size and keep lesser margins between lines.
- If your have old books lying at home, don't throw them away or sell them to the *kabaariwala.* Instead donate them to some library. They can be used by students or avid readers and so this way new books would be printed in a lesser quantity. Also, by doing this, less trees will have to be cut off.
- Use cloth napkins instead of paper napkins. More trees have to be cut down to make paper napkins.
- Share books, magazines, etc., with friends and other known people. This way the consumption of paper is reduced.

Don't waste food while eating

- Take only that much food on your plate that you can eat; don't take excess and then waste it. Remember the poor and hungry who do have food on their plate.

Distribution of old things

- Make it a habit of distributing old things to needy people, maybe on a yearly basis rather than discarding them.

Contribution towards the environment is also national love

- Along with tree planting, water saving, electricity saving, fuel saving, paper saving one should also not use such things that pollutes the atmosphere.
- Whenever you go shopping carry a bag with you – jute bag or cloth bag. Plastic bags are poisonous for the environment because they can't be recycled.
- Safely dispose paints, varnish, kerosene, charcoal, metal cleaners, etc.
- Use organic waste as fertilisers for plants. Avoid chemical fertilisers.
- Reduce bursting crackers for enjoyment. Use of crackers not only wastes money but it is also injurious to health. Experts think that crackers not only create noise pollution but also its smoke mixes with the air and pollutes it. Smoke of crackers contains chemicals, such as sulphur dioxide, nitrogen, suspended particulate matter (SPM) and respirable suspended particulate matter which cause harm to the health in the long run.

Also keep your house pollution free

- There should be a provision for cross ventilation in the house so that fresh air can enter and stale air can escape out.
- Make sure that the exhaust fan in the kitchen is working properly. If possible install an electric chimney in your kitchen to keep your kitchen and house free from kitchen fumes.
- Do not allow anyone to smokes inside your home. If someone has the habit of smoking, he should smoke in the balcony or out in the garden. Special care of this should be taken if there is a new born child at home or there is a

pregnant woman; passive smoking is as harmful as active smoking.

- Throw away empty or half-filled cans of paints and sprays after they have been used, because the chemicals present in them are injurious to health. Keep children away from such poisonous items.
- Save your home from excessive moistness and dampness.
- Keep your entire home clean. Take special care to have a clean kitchen and hygienic bathrooms.
- Curtains, mattresses, pillows, cushions, carpets, door mats, etc., of the entire house should be cleaned or vacuumed at least once a week; they should also be sunned regularly. To protect the pillows from dust, wrap plastic covers on them and then put cloth covers over them.

Do you have ten minutes for your country (An excerpt from the speech of Ex-President Dr. A. P. J. Abdul Kalam)

If you have 10 minutes then read these lines — You say that your government is useless. Rules and regulations have become old, municipality does not lift garbage, phones do not work, railways have become a joke, our airline services are the worst in the world, and postages are never received on time, etc.

You speak, speak, and just speak, but what do you do about it?

Anybody who has been to Singapore will agree with this. You come out of the airport, you have eminent international city in front of you. You don't throw pieces of cigarette butts on the roads. You feel proud of their underground roads that are linked so well. If you have to stay longer than the stipulated time in any restaurant or shopping mall then you have to punch your parking ticket when you return to the parking, whatever your status may be.

In Dubai, during the *Ramzan* days you cannot dare to eat anything publicly. You cannot dare to come out in Jeddah without covering your head. You cannot throw coconut shells anywhere else other than in dustbins at the sea shores of Australia or New Zealand.

Why don't you spit chewed betel (*paan*) on the roads of Tokyo or why don't you take the help of examination brokers to get fake certificates in Boston? It is because you honour the system of government of these countries and obey their rules and regulations.

As soon as you touch Indian soil, you yourself will first throw pieces of paper and cigarette butts on the roads. If you could present yourself as a good citizen in another country then why can't you behave the same in your country, India?

Once Mumbai's Ex-Municipal Commissioner, Sh. Tinnaiker said, that it is the rich and wealthy people who walk their dogs on the roads and leave behind their faeces everywhere and anywhere. And, it is these very people who blame the concerned officers for filth and dirty roads. In America every dog owner has to clean up the mess himself that their pets leave behind. The same rule is followed in Japan also. Will any Indian citizen do the same in India?

We expect the government to do everything for us. Our our contribution remains close to nothing and entirely negative. We expect cleanliness in our cities from the government agencies, but as citizens we continue to throw garbage everywhere around us. We expect the railways to provide us neat and clean coaches and toilets, but we don't want to learn how to use them properly. We expect that Air India provide us the best food available along with world-class facilities, but whenever we get a chance, we don't lose the chance to carry away things from there.

Whenever there is a discussion about solving social problems like dowry and female foeticide, we give big lectures. But, when it comes to putting all that we said into practice we follow just the opposite. In our lives separate rules apply in our homes and separate rules apply to us when we are outside. Aren't we being hypocrites? Dear Indians, this composition is extremely thought-provoking, because it asks us to self-examine ourselves. Here, I want to mention the words that John F. Kennedy said to address his fellow Americans (the words have been changed and have been used in the context of India) – "Ask not what your country can do for you but what you can do for your country." Let us all decide what we can do for our India; and let us do every such thing so that India too can become like America and other western countries. This is what our country expects from all of us. Jai Hind!

Human Religion

Human religion is one that joins one person to another person. It creates love for others, builds respect in the heart of people, brings about brotherhood, and develops politeness for others.

The foundation of religion is the same everywhere, no matter what country, what caste, what colour, or what status one has. Once we are able to understand and believe this then religion will never make us fight each other. It is incorrect to say that disputes take place due to religion. There is no fight due to religion; fights take place due to communal tensions that are manmade. In other words we can say that the main causes of disputes are the sinful acts of the people.

Religion has always worked to bring people together and bond them.

Religion teaches us the art of living life happily by ourselves and letting others live happily too.

If we can't love the people whom we can see then how can we love The Almighty whom we can't see?

Respect others the way you would like them to respect you.

Behave with others the way you would like them to behave with you.

True Asceticism

To renounce your house is not true asceticism.

**To renounce your wife and children and to renounce worldliness and go to the forest
does not mean asceticism.**

True asceticism is to live in your house and perform your duties, and in process of doing everything keep your mind free from tensions, worries, and desires.

Try to fulfil your duties with the feeling of just doing the task rather than having fascinations about them.

Accept everything that is happening to you as the will of

**The Almighty God –
this is true asceticism.**

Self-Realisation

If divine accomplishments are increasing in your life, your mind is getting diverted from sensual enjoyments, it is getting stronger, and happiness is increasing, then you should perceive that you are successively proceeding further on the path of self-realisation. If the influence of evil spirits is increasing in your life, your mind is attracted towards sensual enjoyments, the mind is restlessness and worried, and these continue to increase at a slow or fast pace, then perceive that you are going back in life at that very pace.

Saints or great men preach the world through their way of living not by their language.

Prayer

Prayer is of prime importance in every religion. Praying is the act of trying and getting closer to The almighty to use His support and power to do something good. When we pray then our conscious mind connects with the sub-conscious mind. During this time whatever we visualise is easily accepted by our sub-conscious mind, which then begins to convert that imagination into reality.

Prayer is beneficial, no matter who it is we pray to or pray for. But, when prayers are offered for someone who is not known to us or has no relation with us, the power of prayer increases and we benefit immensely from it.

When we pray in groups then a collective consciousness develops from everybody's self-consciousness. This collective consciousness gets attached to the universal consciousness. That is why group prayer is more effective than personal prayer.

Prayer done for earning good in life is obviously better than that done for collecting material possessions.

Prayers are not always offered to crave worldly desires, but can be presented in thanks and gratitude to the Almighty. When our prayers are immediately answered, they enhance our faith in God; but, there are times when we may have to wait for some time before our prayers are answered. At such a time our patience is put to test. One who can endure this period is a winner in the journey of life.

God never denies anything. He continues to bless us no matter what. Thus, keep the faith alive and never give up.

Liberation

There are four types of desires in human beings – wealth, spirituality or religion, sensual pleasures, and liberation or freedom.

Of these four, wealth and religion both increase each other or it can be said that religion increases wealth and wealth increases religion. But, if religion is followed for indulgence then religion gets destroyed after the fulfilment of one's luxuries, in the same way that wealth if used for indulgence gets destroyed once all worldly desires are fulfilled. Thus, it can be said that indulgence destroys both wealth and spirituality.

Following a spiritual life purifies the inner soul and frees it and leads to liberation. In the same way if wealth is used for the benefit, welfare, and happiness of others, it too leads to liberation and cleansing of the soul. Though the objective of spirituality and liberation are different, both use the human body as a means to attain their goal. To fulfil our spiritual goal we use the body to meditate and perform religious ceremonies, and to attain liberation from worldly desires our emotions and thoughts play a major role. Nothing is absolute in life, except death. Life is ever-changing – seasons come and go as do grief and pleasure that come and go as waves in our lives. The coming and going of circumstances is a perpetual rule of this world. The one who understands this perpetual rule is liberated forever, free from life's imprisonment and shackles.

Not to get influenced or deviated by anything worldly is true liberation.

Books by Dr. Brij Bhushan Goel

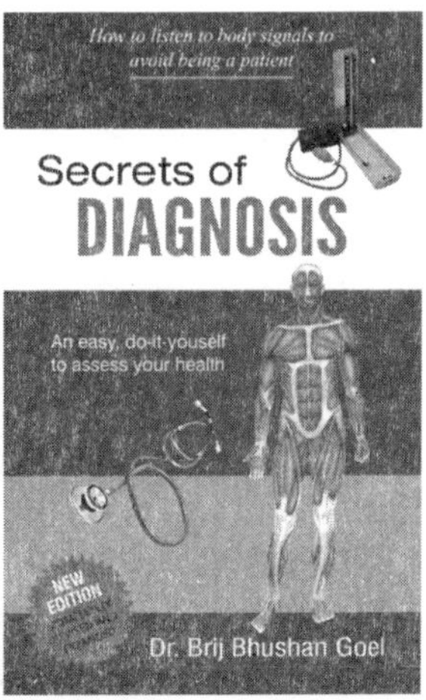

For catalogue write to:

Sterling Publishers (P) Ltd.
A-59, Okhla Industrial Area,
Phase-II, New Delhi-110020.
Tel: 26387070, 26386209;
Fax: 91-11-26383788
E-mail: mail@sterlingpublishers.com
www.sterlingpublishers.com